500 prints
on clay

500 prints on clay

An Inspiring Collection of Image Transfer Work

Paul Andrew Wandless, Juror

LARK
CRAFTS
Asheville

EDITOR
Linda Kopp

PRODUCTION EDITOR
Julie Hale

ART DIRECTOR
Matt Shay

COVER DESIGNER
Shannon Yokeley

FRONT COVER, CLOCKWISE FROM LEFT
Matt L. Conlon
Untitled, 2011

Israel Shawn Davis
Yunomi Series: Here's to the Birthday Boy Dreaming, 2011

Keri Straka
Cellular, 2011

Jason Bige Burnett
Carnival Wall Tiles, 2010

BACK COVER, CLOCKWISE FROM LEFT
Claire Tietje
White-Crowned Sparrow Bottle with Stopper, 2010

Jill Oberman
Bloom, 2010

Ulrika Jarl
Globalization—Willow Pattern Reinterpreted, 2010

Charlie Cummings
Stratospheric Vase, 2007

Douglas E. Gray
Scandalous Tweets: Self Made, 2011

SPINE
Nathan Falter
Gas Can, 2011

FRONT FLAP
Michael T. Schmidt
Gulf and BP Teabowls, 2010

BACK FLAP
Aaron Michael Calvert
Industrious Ant Teapot, 2009

TITLE PAGE
Shamai Sam Gibsh
Stelae, 2011

OPPOSITE
Dana Childs
Contrapposto, 2009

LARK CRAFTS

An Imprint of Sterling Publishing
387 Park Avenue South
New York, NY 10016

If you have questions or comments
about this book, please visit: larkcrafts.com

Library of Congress Cataloging-in-Publication Data

500 prints on clay : an inspiring collection of image transfer work. -- First Edition.

pages cm

ISBN 978-1-4547-0331-0

1. Transfer-printing. I. Title: Showcase five hundred prints on clay.

NK4607.S56 2013

769.9'051--dc23

2012020920

10 9 8 7 6 5 4 3 2 1

First Edition

Published by Lark Crafts
An Imprint of Sterling Publishing Co., Inc.
387 Park Avenue South, New York, NY 10016

Text © 2013, Lark Crafts, an Imprint of Sterling Publishing Co., Inc.
Photography © 2013, Artist/Photographer

Distributed in Canada by Sterling Publishing,
c/o Canadian Manda Group, 165 Dufferin Street
Toronto, Ontario, Canada M6K 3H6

Distributed in the United Kingdom by GMC Distribution Services,
Castle Place, 166 High Street, Lewes, East Sussex, England BN7 1XU

Distributed in Australia by Capricorn Link (Australia) Pty Ltd.,
P.O. Box 704, Windsor, NSW 2756 Australia

Manufactured in China

ISBN 13: 978-1-4547-0331-0

For information about custom editions, special sales, and premium and corporate purchases, please contact Sterling Special Sales Department at 800-805-5489 or specialsales@sterlingpub.com.

Requests for information about desk and examination copies available to college and university professors must be submitted to academic@larkbooks.com. Our complete policy can be found at www.larkcrafts.com.

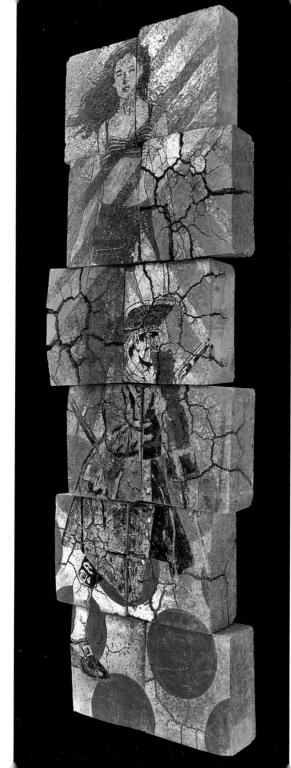

contents

introduction

500 Prints on Clay is the first survey dedicated to artwork created through the union of ceramic techniques and printmaking methods. The two mediums have long been combined to make art, but their pairing hasn't always enjoyed the attention it's rightfully receiving today. Now seen and recognized in more exhibitions and publications than ever before, printed ceramic pieces bring together the best of both artistic genres, blending tradition and innovation in ways that indicate an exciting future for the world of clay.

As the book's juror, I had the opportunity to view thousands of varied and sophisticated works made by artists from around the world. The pieces either incorporated image-transfer techniques or were fully executed with those methods, and as a result, they constitute a separate genre, one that isn't specifically about clay or printmaking but something in between. This space in between is a very large area in which artists are now working creatively, producing a kind of hybrid art that challenges the ways we think about ceramics. Although the genre has roots in two different worlds, it nevertheless occupies its own artistic ground.

Clay prints using obvious printmaking methods are often perceived simply as clay versions of what can be executed on paper. But this perception ignores the ways in which clay materials

FRANK JAMES FISHER
American Home ■ 2011

recontextualize the printed image, giving it a unique appearance that's only possible through the vehicle of clay. There's a distinctiveness to what can be accomplished with ceramic finishes and firing methods that paper and ink just can't duplicate. At the same time, of course, the images, patterns, and designs that can now be featured in clay are only available through the use of printmaking tools. This special blend of strengths is what makes the work on these pages so exceptional.

Artists working within the genre use painting, photography, and digital software as embellishment, along with embossing, screening, monoprinting, and paper transfers. They create work that's visually unique by exploiting the potential of image, design pattern, and text on a clay surface. That surface could be a flat tile, a nonobjective sculpture, a figurative piece, or a vessel. It could be an outdoor mural or a conceptual installation. Because image-transfer

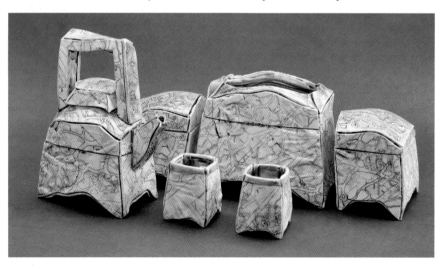

MARC J. BARR
Tea Set 196 ■ 2010

techniques can be incorporated into any kind of work, ceramists don't have to change the kind of art they make in order to use them; they simply get to add to their options for surface design.

Flip through these pages, and you'll find work exploring a wide range of themes, including nature, mortality, and relationships. In order to enhance their concepts or enrich the narrative nature of their work, artists use everything from chunks of text and photographs to hand-drawn illustrations and custom-made decals. In his embossed piece *American Home*, Frank James Fisher employs a symbolic structure as a canvas for vintage ads, old logos, and visuals from discarded printing plates.

MEREDITH HOST
Dot Dot Dash Tumblers ■ 2011

The result is a sly commentary on consumerism and the culture of the modern family.

Many artists play with familiar forms, providing fresh perspectives on everyday objects. With its off-kilter contours and pronounced sense of texture, Marc J. Barr's *Tea Set 196* is a wonderfully original take on the traditional cup-and-vessel ensemble. Meredith Host (*Dot Dot Dash Tumblers*) and Colin John Klimesh (*Stemless Wine Glass,* page 163) apply a contemporary aesthetic to utilitarian vessels, favoring retro graphics and layered motifs.

Other ceramists use image-transfer methods to create pieces that exhibit a bold visual splendor. Maria Esther Barbieri's hypnotic *Jorop Art* spellbinds viewers with its intricate design, while the complex surface pattern of Avital Sheffer's *Shefah VI* (page 47) draws us in for a closer look.

As these artists so beautifully demonstrate, the combination of clay processes and printmaking methods represents a natural, logical evolution of both mediums. As technological advancements in both areas continue to grow, so will the range of work.

My involvement with this book has been a real privilege. The field of submissions was extremely rich, and narrowing it down to fit within the confines of this volume was very difficult. The level of experimentation that's taking place as artists explore the combination of two timeless mediums is remarkable. These artists—or clay printers—are merging processes and tools to express themselves in ways that are innovative and new. This book is a gallery of truly inspiring work—art that's visually dynamic, technically challenging, and intellectually engaging. I hope you enjoy the journey of discovering this new creative territory.

— Paul Andrew Wandless

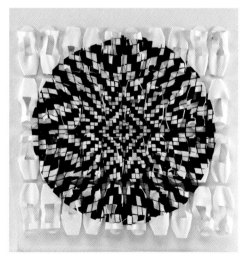

MARIA ESTHER BARBIERI
Jorop Art ■ 2009

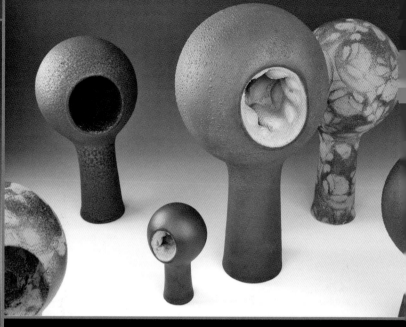

the pieces

GRACIELA OLIO
Proyecto Sur, Home Series #65 ■ 2011
5 x 4 x 5½ inches (12.7 x 10.2 x 14 cm)
Hand-built sheet porcelain; fired,
cone 8, photo-ceramic print using
gum bichromate process
PHOTO BY ARTIST

ELIZABETH FARSON
Polly Oil Can ■ 2011

12 x 6 x 10 inches (30.5 x 15.2 x 25.4 cm)
Slab can, press-molded top, thrown spout, wire
handle, decal; impressed, rolled assembled, cone
10 clay bisqued to 05, glazed, raku fired, cone 07
PHOTO BY ARTIST

OFRA AMIKAM
Finjan Bar in Blue ■ 2011
9 x 10 inches (22.9 x 25.4 cm)
Earthenware clay, ceramic decals, gold luster;
slip cast, electric fired, cone 04 glaze
PHOTO BY ARTIST

DAVID SCOTT BOGUS
The Optimist Luggage 12 ■ 2011
16 x 16 x 8 inches (40.6 x 40.6 x 20.3 cm)
Slip-cast white earthenware; multiple fired,
cone 06-018, luster, overglaze decal
PHOTO BY ARTIST

13

NAN SMITH
Summer's Over ■ 2011
62½ x 2½ x 59½ inches (158.8 x 64.8 x 151.1 cm)
Earthenware clay, sand, paint, plastic, wood, glaze with china-paint
photographic decals; multiple fired, cone 03 bisque, cone 06 glaze,
cone 018 decal firing, photographs composited using Photoshop
PHOTOS BY ALLEN CHEUVRONT

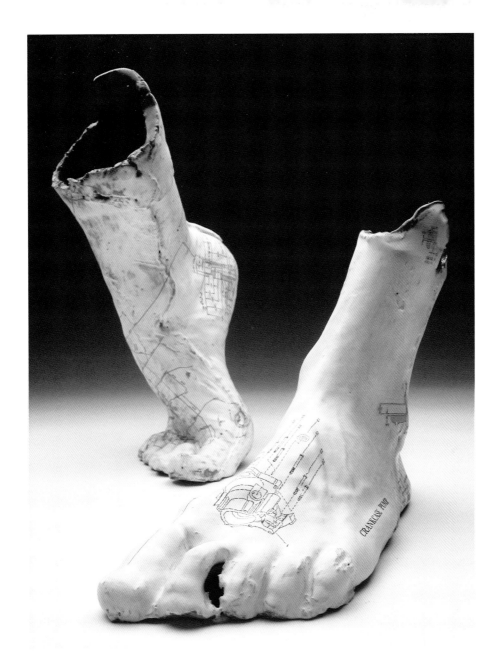

FREDERICK A. BARTOLOVIC
Crankcase Pump ■ 2006
15 x 10 x 15 inches (38.1 x 25.4 x 38.1 cm)
Stoneware clay, iron-oxide decals;
multiple fired, cone 04-6

ARTHUR PADILLA GONZALEZ
Good Sam with Chaos ■ 2011
12 x 12 inches (30.5 x 30.5 cm)
Earthenware clay; single fired, cone 2,
underglaze, monoprint from plaster slab
PHOTO BY KATHERINE WALTERS

SHAE BISHOP
Apocalypse ■ 2010
9 x 6½ inches (22.9 x 16.5 cm)
White earthenware, gold luster; underglaze,
clear glaze, monoprint from plaster slab
PHOTO BY JIM WALKER

17

DAVID L. GAMBLE
From the Manhole Cover Series: Diptych ■ 2006
Each piece: 14 x 11 inches (35.6 x 27.9 cm)
Terra cotta; bisque fired, cone 03, hand built, direct print,
cropped, glaze over copper-oxide wash, electric fired, cone 04
PHOTO BY ARTIST

500
prints on clay

MATT L. CONLON
Untitled ■ 2011
6¼ x 4½ x 1½ inches (15.9 x 11.4 x 3.8 cm)
Porcelain; soda fired, cone 11, intaglio
PHOTOS BY ARTIST

19

MELISSA TERREZZA
Bang ■ 2011
27 x 15 inches (68.6 x 38.1 cm)
Low-fire casting slip; cone 04, underglaze,
screen-printed, image transfer
PHOTO BY LYNNE HARTY

HANNAH E. LEVIN
Little Bird Dress Vase ■ 2010
9 1/2 x 7 1/2 x 5 inches (24.1 x 19.1 x 12.7 cm)
Wheel-thrown and altered clay,
decals; cone 6, hand carved
PHOTO BY ROBERT LEVIN

RICHARD LAWSON
Raku with Carp ■ 2010
10 3/4 x 7 1/2 inches (27.3 x 19.1 cm)
Laguna B-Mix; transfers fired on greenware,
raku fired with glazes, cone 06
PHOTO BY ARTIST

LISA PAGE MAHER
Hummer Cup ■ 2011
6 x 3 inches (15.2 x 7.6 cm)
Terra cotta; Chinese underglaze
decals, underglazes, clear glaze;
cone 05 white slip, electric fired
PHOTO BY MICHAEL C. MAHER

23

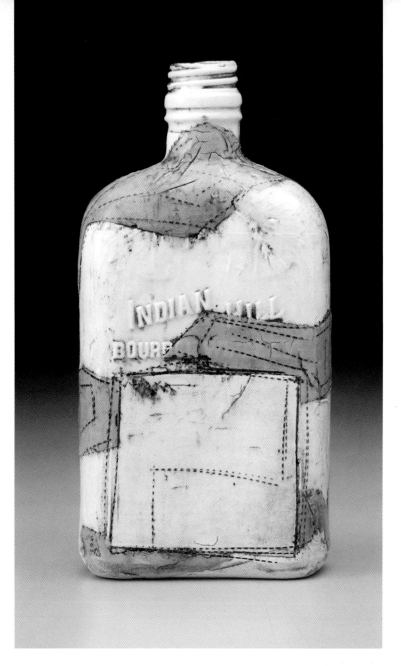

THOM O'HEARN
Bourbon Bottle #4 ■ 2011
8 x 5 x 1½ inches (20.3 x 12.7 x 3.8 cm)
Stoneware clay; multiple fired, cone 06-6,
cast object and relief, one-color slip-transfer
print, traced lines, underglaze, glaze
PHOTO BY STEVE MANN

FACING PAGE
SAM SCOTT
Nation Building ■ 2006
12 inches (30.5 cm) in diameter
Kai porcelain; fired, cone 12,
wheel thrown, stamped, stained
with black underglaze
PHOTO BY ARTIST

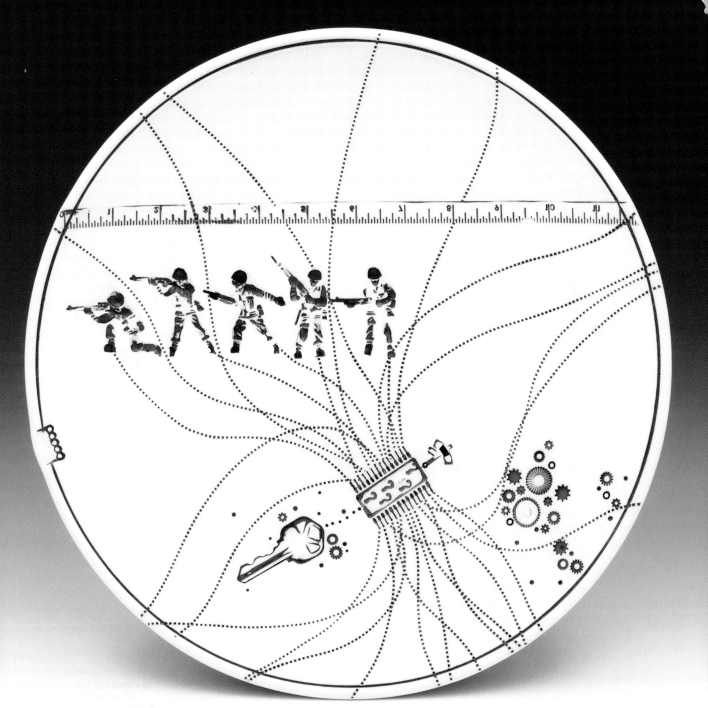

TODD SHANAFELT
Pneumatic ■ 2010
13¹/₂ x 14¹/₂ x 9 inches (34.3 x 36.8 x 22.9 cm)
Earthenware, metal, rubber, ceramic decal,
ceramic tile; multiple fired, cones 03 and 018
PHOTO BY ARTIST

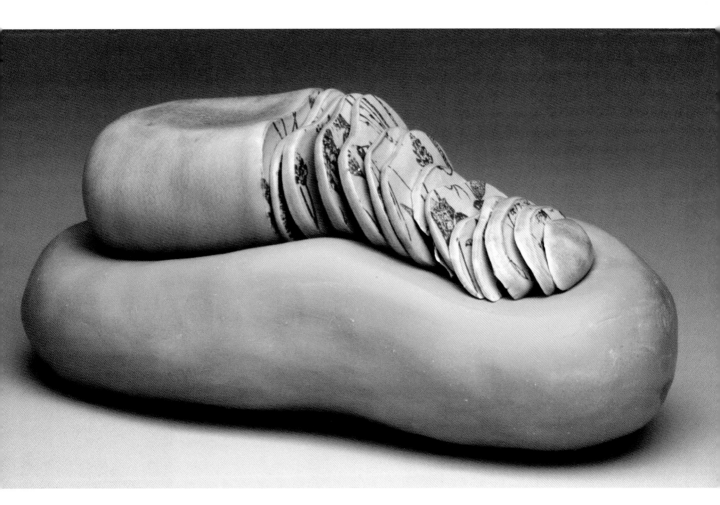

AMY CHASE
Interruption ■ 2011
4 x 7½ inches (10.2 x 19.1 cm)
Porcelain, terra cotta; reduction fired, cone 10,
cone 04, silk-screened underglaze decals
PHOTO BY ARTIST

ALFREDO EANDRADE
Communicating Vessels (Vasos Comunicantes) ■ 2010
52 x 35 x 39 inches (132.1 x 88.9 x 99.1 cm)
Earthenware clay; multiple fired, cone 4, underglaze,
image transfer from laser photocopy
PHOTO BY DAMIÁN WASSER

JEN GANDEE
Formation ■ 2008
48 x 24 x 84 inches (121.9 x 61 x 213.4 cm)
Wheel-thrown vessels; screen-printed
underglaze tranfers

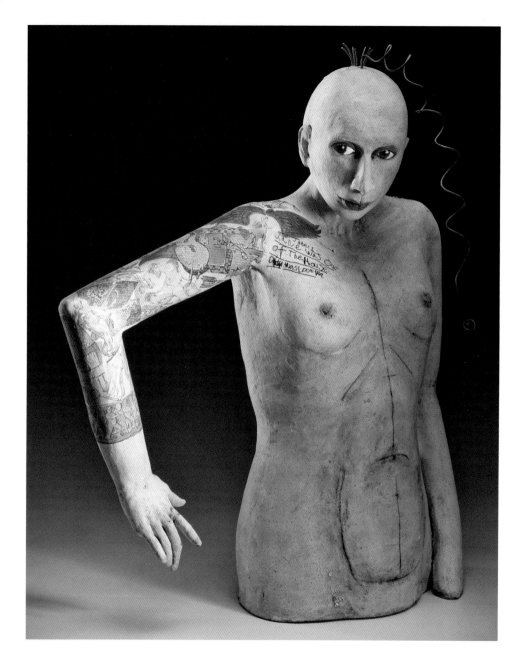

NANCY KUBALE
Wing ■ 2009
24 x 12 x 8 inches (61 x 30.5 x 20.3 cm)
Stoneware clay, handmade laser-printed
decals; multiple fired, cone 04, terra sigillata,
underglaze, oxide, hand colored
PHOTO BY ROBERT BATEY

EVA LAPKA
Whispers ■ 2009
Each: 9 x 8 x 6 inches (22.9 x 20.3 x 15.2 cm)
Stoneware clay; cone 6, underglaze, glaze
PHOTO BY PHOTOGRAPHOS INC.

ROBYN HOSKING
HMAS Second Craft Citizens ■ 2010
6 1/2 x 13 x 6 inches (16.5 x 33 x 15.2 cm)
Stoneware slip, porcelain slip, ceramic
decals and lusters; underglaze, multiple
fired, cone 018-7, slip cast, hand altered
PHOTO BY NICK KREISLER

CALDER KAMIN
Uncover Unconscious ■ 2007
36 x 24 x 6 inches (91.4 x 61 x 15.2 cm)
White earthenware; casting slip,
cone 04, monoprint underglaze
PHOTO BY JEFF BRUCE

33

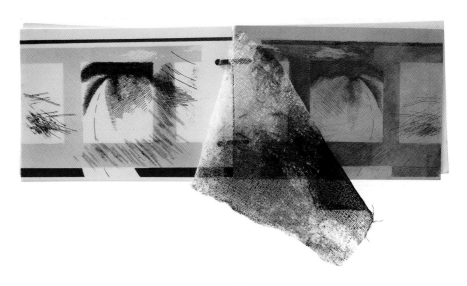

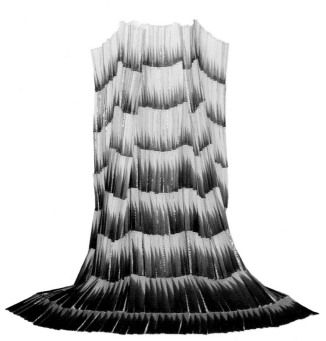

PIET STOCKMANS
Object Inspired by the Plumed Coat
of Montezuma, XVI Century ■ 2007
80 x 80 inches (203.2 x 203.2 cm)
Slip-cast unglazed porcelain; cone 14
PHOTO BY ARTIST

LAURA SCOPA
Istantanea ■ 2011
8 5/8 x 19 11/16 inches (22 x 50 cm)
Engraved clay; fired, oxide
PHOTO BY ARTIST

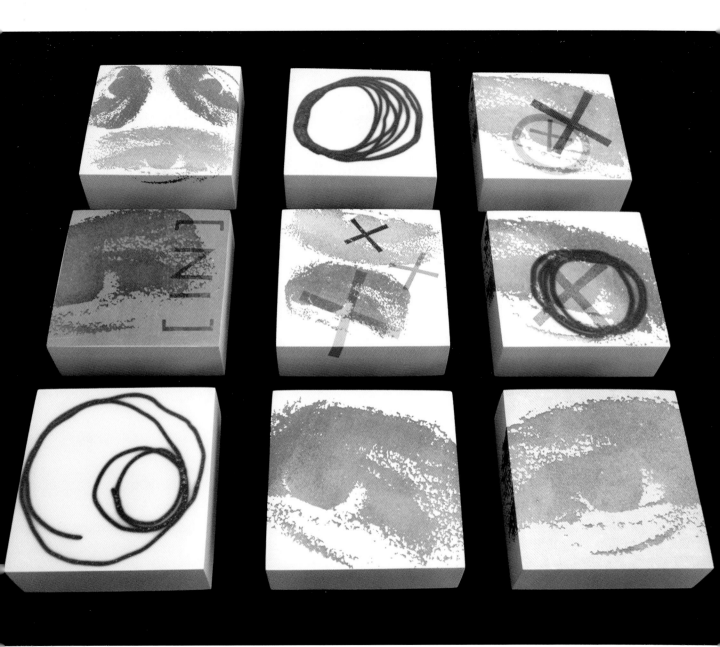

MARC VERBRUGGEN
Signals of Life: Composition III ■ 2011
19 ¹¹/₁₆ x 19 ¹¹/₁₆ inches (50 x 50 cm)
Hand-formed white casting clay, copper wire,
decals; cast, sgrafitto, terra sigillata, gas fired
in oxidation, electric fired in oxidation
PHOTO BY ARTIST

35

HONG-LING WEE
Chinese Zodiac Bowls ■ 2011
Each: 2 x 4 x 4 inches (5.1 x 10.2 x 10.2 cm)
Porcelain, in-glaze decals; high fired, cone 6
PHOTO BY ARTIST

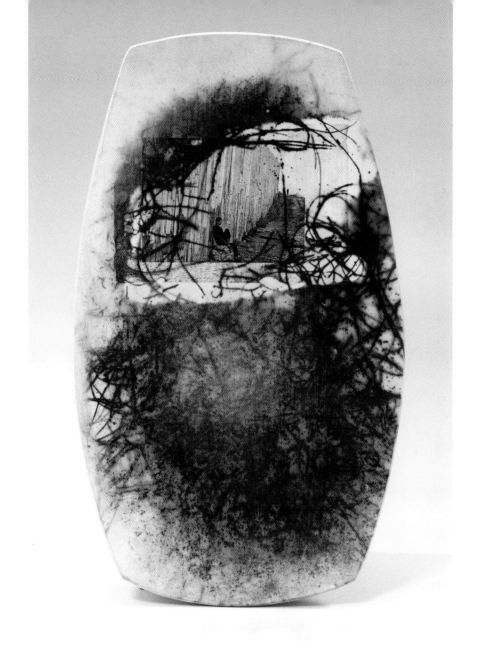

SHAMAI SAM GIBSH
Stela-3 ■ 2011
17 x 10 x ³/₁₆ inches (43.2 x 25.4 x 0.5 cm)
Stoneware clay, laser-iron decal; terra
sigillata, saggar fired in reduction
with organic material, cone 07
PHOTO BY ARTIST

37

SUSAN FEAGIN
Decorative Tea Set ■ 2011

Teapot: 6 1/2 x 11 1/2 x 4 1/2 inches (16.5 x 29.2 x 11.5 cm)
Cups: 3 1/4 x 4 1/2 inches (8.2 x 11.4 cm) each
Mid-range porcelain; oxidation fired, cone 7, screen-
printed colored slip and underglaze sgraffito
PHOTO BY WALKER MONTGOMERY

TIFFANY SCHMIERER
Bay Views I ■ 2011
23 x 16 x 10 inches (58.4 x 40.6 x 25.4 cm)
Sculpture clay; multiple fired, cone 06-1, painted,
stenciled, silk-screened, underglaze, glaze
PHOTO BY WILFRED J. JONES

39

CLAIRE TIETJE
Song Sparrow Tumblers ■ 2011

Each: 4 1/2 x 3 1/4 x 3 1/4 inches (11.4 x 8.3 x 8.3 cm)
Slab-built porcelain; carved and impressed
with chopstick, cone 5 oxidation, digital-image
transfer, underglaze, colored slip, clear glaze
PHOTO BY ARTIST

KELLY MCKIBBEN HARRO
Untitled ■ 2011
5¹/₂ x 12 x 3¹/₂ inches (14 x 30.5 x 8.9 cm)
Earthenware clay; cone 04, screen-printed slips
PHOTO BY ARTIST

JASON BIGE BURNETT
Carnival Wall Tiles ■ 2010
Each: 9¼ x 5½ x 2 inches (23.5 x 14 x 5.1 cm)
Earthenware clay, iron oxide and commercial decals, luster;
screen-printed slips, newsprint transfer, multiple fired
PHOTO BY MARISA FALCIGNO

AMY CHASE
Reassurance ■ 2010

6 x 20 inches (15.2 x 50.8 cm)
Porcelain; reduction fired, cone 10,
silk-screened underglaze decals
PHOTO BY ARTIST

DENISE LYNN RUSSELL
Vintage Dresses II ■ 2011
10 x 8 x 3 inches (25.4 x 20.3 x 7.6 cm)
Polymer clay, newsprint paper,
varnish veneer; oven baked
PHOTO BY ARTIST

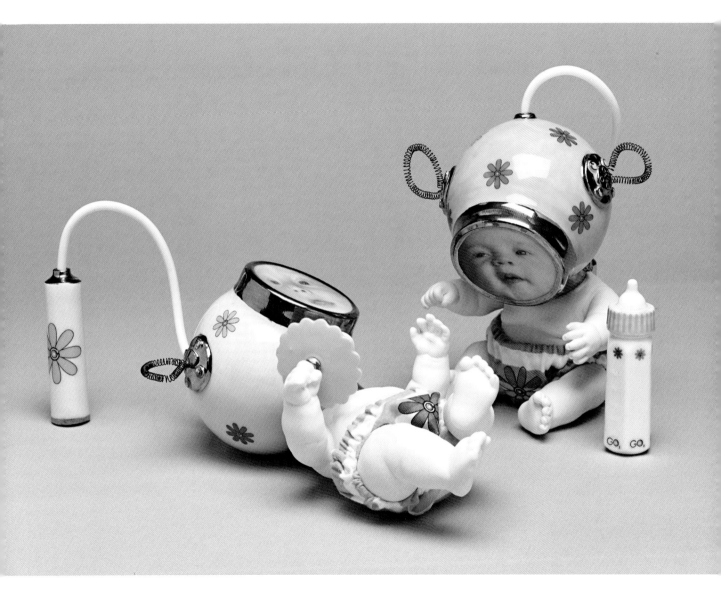

ROBYN HOSKING
Go Oxygen for Happy, Healthy Babies ■ 2010
Each: 7½ x 10 x 9 inches (19.1 x 25.4 x 22.9 cm)
Cool Ice Porcelain slip, colored porcelain slips, ceramic decals
and lusters; multiple fired, cone 018-5, slip cast, hand altered
PHOTO BY JEREMY DILLION

GARRY JOHN BISH
Still Life: I Had a Word ■ 2008
29 1/8 x 21 13/16 inches (74 x 55.5 cm)
Press-molded stoneware; slip ground with
single-color silk-screened decal in black enamel
PHOTO BY IAN HILL

AVITAL SHEFFER
Shefah VI ■ 2011
11 x 16 x 7½ inches (27.9 x 40.6 x 19.1 cm)
Earthenware clay, engobes; glazes,
screen-printed, multiple fired, cone 04
PHOTO BY DAVID YOUNG

SHAMAI SAM GIBSH
Stelae ■ 2011
97 x 90 x 23 inches (246.4 x 228.6 x 58.4 cm)
Stoneware clay, laser-iron decal, sand; terra sigillata,
saggar fired in reduction with organic material, cone 07
PHOTO BY RON ARDA

TERRIE BANHAZL
Wave Tile ■ 2011
6½ x 9½ inches (15.5 x 24.2 cm)
Hand-carved stoneware clay, china paint;
glaze, cone 5, laser-printer transfer
PHOTO BY ARTIST

49

ARTHUR PADILLA GONZALEZ
I Envy Your Greed ■ 2010
19 x 35 x 3 inches (48.3 x 88.9 x 7.6 cm)
Earthenware clay, Egyptian paste; single fired, cone 1,
underglaze, monoprint with raku and majolica glaze elements
PHOTO BY JOHN WILSON WHITE

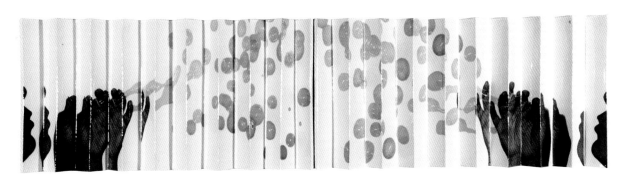

BRIAN JON BOLDON
Echo ■ 2011
10 x 40 inches (25.4 x 101.6 cm)
Earthenware clay, laser-printed digital ceramic
decals; multiple fired, cones 02, 04, 010
PHOTO BY ARTIST

ELLEN MULLIGAN
Sadie and Her Chicken Platter ■ 2010
6 x 15½ inches (2.5 x 15.2 x 39.4 cm)
Porcelain clay, image from original artwork;
cone 6, gocco screen, wax resist, glaze sgrafitto
PHOTO BY ARTIST

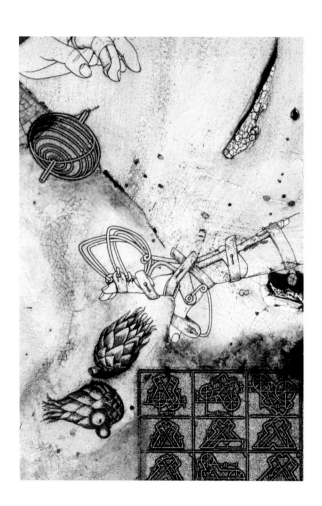

KAREN M. GUNDERMAN
Dexterity (Panel 2) ■ 1998
33 x 20 inches (83.8 x 50.8 cm)
Castable refractory; cone 10 with porcelain
slip, screen-printed stains and underglazes
PHOTOS BY ARTIST

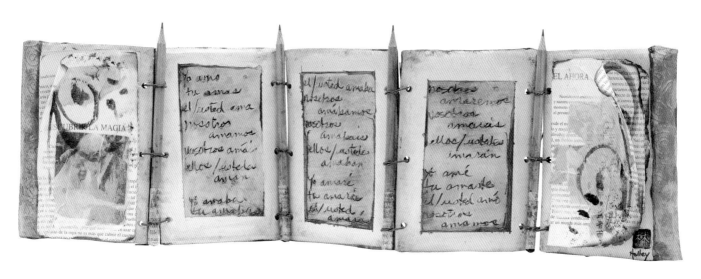

LIN M. HOLLEY
El Mundo Sagrado ■ 2010
6 x 20 x 5 inches (15.2 x 50.8 x 12.7 cm)
Hand and slab-built earthenware clay, book pages, found
objects, acrylic paint, cold-finish patinas; multiple fired,
cone 04-06, underglazes and cone 06 glazes, collaged
PHOTOS BY KEN WAGNER

ADRIENNE SPEER
Bowl with Bird and Roses ■ 2011

7½ x 5½ x 2 inches (19.1 x 14 x 5.1 cm)
Slab-built earthenware; electric fired, cone
05, sgraffito, underglazes, painted and
stamped with hand-carved rubber stamps
PHOTO BY ARTIST

CHARLOTTE STOCKLEY
Meat and Two Veg Plate ■ 2011

11 inches (27.9 cm) in diameter
Thrown stoneware clay; cone 6,
lithographic print, transparent glaze
PHOTO BY ARTIST

RENA HAMILTON
Vintage Revolver Lunchware ■ 2011
Mug: 4¼ x 5 x 3¾ inches (10.8 x 12.7 x 8.3 cm)
Plate: 9 inches (22.9 cm) in diameter
Bowl: 3 x 6 x 6 inches (7.6 x 15.2 x 15.2 cm)
Earthenware; oxidation fired, cone 05; silk-screened, transferred underglaze decal

HENNIE MEYER
ICU ■ 2011
$31\frac{1}{2}$ x $31\frac{1}{2}$ x $4\frac{11}{16}$ images (80 x 80 x 12 cm)
Earthenware clay, enamel; cone 5,
oxide, monoprint, onglaze color
PHOTO BY ARTIST

JEANNE OPGENHAFFEN
Boxes ■ 2011
Each: 3⁷/₈ x 2 x 2 inches (9.8 x 5.1 x 5.1 cm)
Porcelain, decals; multiple fired, screen-printed
PHOTO BY S. VAN HUL

MARY ELIZABETH ENGEL
Bird Dog ∎ 2010
14 x 10 x 7 inches (35.6 x 25.4 x 17.8 cm)
Earthenware clay, decals, found objects;
multiple fired, cone 04-07
PHOTO BY CARLO NASISSE

ANTONELLA CIMATTI
Fiori-Frutta ■ 2007
11½ x 4½ inches (29.2 x 11.5 cm)
Earthenware clay, majolica, digital decal;
multiple fired, cones 08, 09, and 010, overglaze
PHOTO BY RAFFAELE TASSINARI

SHARI BRAY
Summer ■ 2011
8 x 9½ inches (20.3 x 24.2 cm)
Raku clay with porcelain slip surface coat; bisque
fired, cone 04, underglazes, screen-printed
PHOTO BY KELLY MCCLENDON

500
prints on clay

STEPHEN L. HORN
Above and Below ■ 2008

10 x 8 x 1 inches (25.4 x 20.3 x 2.5 cm)
Stoneware clay; glaze firing, cone 6,
toner transfer to plastic clay
PHOTO BY SCOTT BRINEGAR

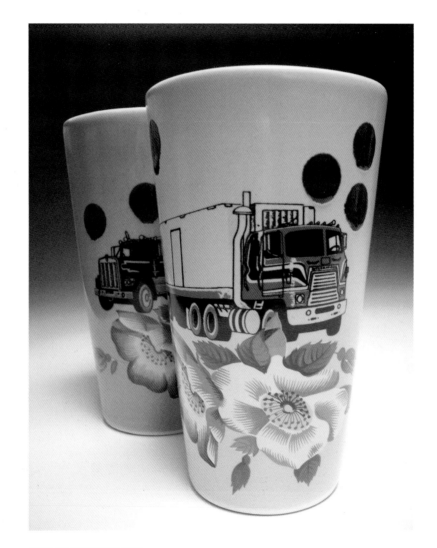

AMY SANTOFERRARO
Trucker Cups ■ 2009

Each: 7 x 3 x 3 inches (17.8 x 7.6 x 7.6 cm)
Slip-cast porcelain; multiple glaze firing,
multiple decal firing
PHOTO BY ARTIST

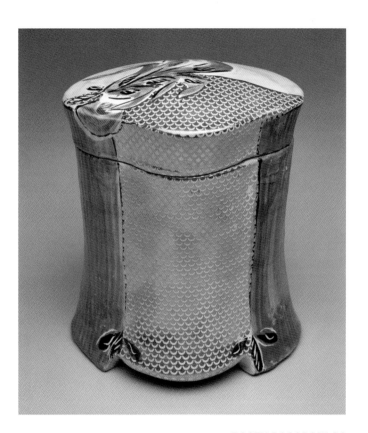

POSEY BACOPOULOS
Oval Box ■ 2010
6 x 6 x 3½ inches (15.2 x 15.2 x 8.9 cm)
Earthenware clay; multiple fired,
cones 06, 04, and 018
PHOTO BY KEVIN NOBEL

RIMAS VISGIRDA
I Could Have Danced All Night... ■ 2011
7½ x 5 x 5 inches (19.1 x 12.7 x 12.7 cm)
Porcelain with granite, self-made and open-stock
decals, gold luster; thrown, wood fired, glazed,
fired, cone 05, multiple fired, cone 016, overglazes
PHOTO BY ARTIST

63

MELISSA TERREZZA
Bloom ■ 2011

16 x 22 inches (40.6 x 55.9 cm)
Low-fire casting slip; cone 04, underglaze,
screen-printed, image transfer
PHOTO BY LYNNE HARTY

ROBIN P. DEBRECENI
Serendipity ■ 2011
17 x 11 inches (43.2 x 27.9 cm)
Clay, universal pigments; clay monoprint
PHOTO BY JOHN IGNARRI

MERYL RUTH
Mel-Oh-Tea-Us, a Ceramic Teapot ■ 2010
18 x 9½ x 4½ inches (45.7 x 24.2 x 11.5 cm)
Slab-constructed stoneware clay, china
paints; multiple fired, cones 06, 5/6, and 015,
underglaze, one-color photo silk-screening
PHOTOS BY BERNARD BLAIS

500
prints on clay

DALIA LAUČKAITĖ-JAKIMAVIČIENĖ
Lamp ■ 2011
6¹³/₁₆ x 3¹¹/₁₆ x 2½ inches (17.3 x 9.4 x 6.4 cm)
Porcelain, decals, electric light; glaze, gas
fired, cone 11, cone 01, silk-screened decals,
overglaze colors, lusters, cone 016
PHOTO BY VIDMANTAS ILČIUKAS

NANCY D. HERMAN
Frankenfood Takeout ■ 2011
4 x 10 x 10 inches (10.2 x 25.4 x 25.4 cm)
Hand-built porcelain, laser-toner
decals; cast, underglaze, cone 06
PHOTO BY TIM BARNWELL

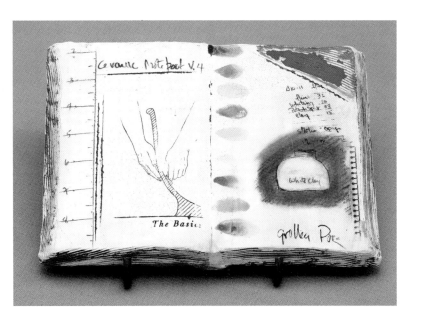

NANCY SELVIN
Notebook Vol. 4 ■ 2009
7 1/2 x 11 inches (19.1 x 27.9 cm)
Terra-cotta paper clay; underglaze, screened,
mishima, sgrafitto, underglaze pencil, cone 1

KERI STRAKA
Cushion and Pins ■ 2011
6 x 8 x 6 inches (15.2 x 20.3 x 15.2 cm)
Porcelain clay, metal pins; lithographic printing,
ceramic-stain washes, cone 6, oxidation fired

MARY F. FISCHER
Western Wool and Mohair ■ 2011
11 x 12 x 4 inches (27.9 x 30.5 x 10.2 cm)
Stoneware clay, mason stains, laser copy; multiple
fired, cone 06-5, image transfer, crackle glaze
PHOTO BY ANSON SEALE

GREG KINNEY
The Letter Home ■ 2009
10¼ x 6 x 6 inches (26 x 15.2 x 15.2 cm)
Earthenware, manganese wash, laser decals;
multiple fired, cone 04-06, underglazes
PHOTO BY ARTIST

MICHAEL KIFER
Wall Slab ■ 2009

14 x 19 inches (35.6 x 48.3 cm)
Hand-built white earthenware; sprayed,
brushed, underglaze decoration with patina
PHOTO BY LARRY SANDERS

SHARON VIRTUE
Clay Poems: Four Small Squares ◼ 2010
Each: 6 x 6 x ½ inches (15.2 x 15.2 x 1.3 cm)
Earthenware clay; multiple fired, cones 1 and 07, printed
with texture and images, underglazes, translucent glazes
PHOTO BY ARTIST

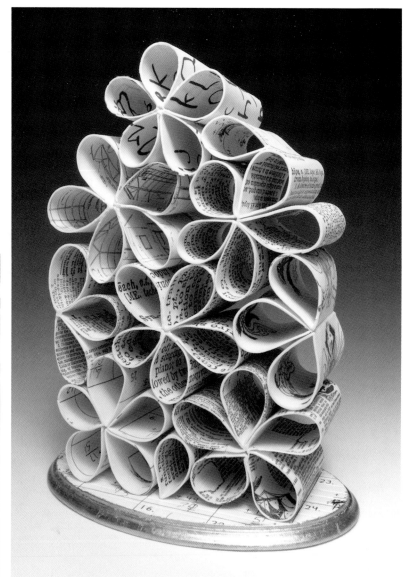

LESLEY BAKER
Untitled ■ 2009
12 x 9 x 5 inches (30.5 x 22.9 x 12.7 cm)
Hand-built and slip-cast porcelain, laser
decals, gold leaf; multiple fired, cone 01-6
PHOTOS BY ARTIST

JEANNE OPGENHAFFEN
Justice-Unjustice ■ 2011
43 5/16 x 43 5/16 inches (110 x 110 cm)
Porcelain, decals; screen-printed
PHOTOS BY S. VAN HUL

JASNA SOKOLOVIC
Dancing with Myself ■ 2010
Each: 12 9/16 inches (32 cm) tall
Earthenware clay, red thread; cone 4, underglazes,
glazes, stenciled, silk-screened, ceramic pencil
PHOTO BY ARTIST

STEPHANIE NICOLE MARTIN
Untitled ■ 2011
20 x 7 x 5 inches (50.8 x 17.8 x 12.7 cm)
Earthenware, laser decals;
cone 04, underglaze, slips
PHOTO BY JUAN VILLA

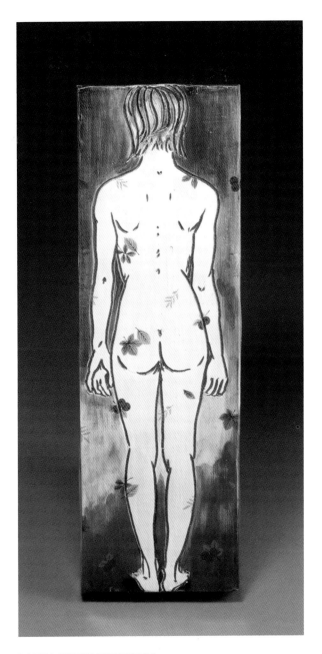

LAURA MARIE O'DONNELL
Curtain (Cherries Jubilee) ■ 2007
17 x 5½ x 1½ inches (43.2 x 14 x 3.8 cm)
Hand-built earthenware clay, ceramic decals; slip,
underglaze, glaze, multiple fired, cones 017 and 04
PHOTO BY BRYAN HEATON

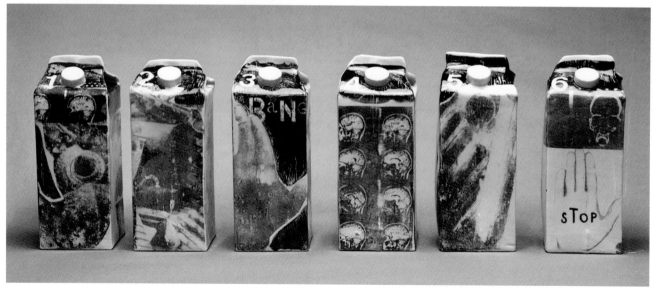

KRISTINA BOGDANOV-ILIC
Iconoclast ■ 2008
Each: 12 x 4 x 4 inches (30.5 x 10.2 x 10.2 cm)
Cast porcelain; glazed, cone 6, underglaze,
photolithography image transfer, stenciled
PHOTOS BY ARTIST

STEPHEN EDGAR HEYWOOD
Bottles ■ 2007
15 x 16 x 10 inches (38.1 x 40.6 x 25.4 cm)
Stoneware; wood fired, cone 10, slip stenciled
PHOTO BY ARTIST

PAULINE JOY MONKCOM

Thames ◼ 2011

17 x 17½ x 2 inches (43.2 x 44.5 x 5.1 cm)
Red earthenware clay; terra sigillata slip,
reduced luster glazes, cone 6, multiple fired,
silk-screen transfer print, latex and paper resist

PHOTO BY ARTIST

DOROTHY SEGAL
Port Marly, 1896 ■ 2011
5½ x 5½ x ¼ inches (14 x 14 x 0.6 cm)
Porcelain, red-iron oxide decal;
fired, cone 10, fired, cone 04
PHOTO BY ARTIST

EVA KWONG
Red and Black Bacteria Cups ■ 2008
Left: 4 x 3½ inches (10.2 x 8.9 cm)
Right: 4½ x 3½ inches (11.4 x 8.9 cm)
Porcelain, decals made from original drawings;
cone 6, glaze, overglaze, silk-screened
PHOTO BY DONG-JUN SHIN

DIANE C. DUVALL
Southern Gravy Boat ■ 2010
5½ x 11½ x 3½ inches (14 x 29.2 x 8.9 cm)
Post-consumer ware; on-glaze decal, cone 018
PHOTO BY DURGA GARCIA

JENNY HODGE
The Phantom: Tassy Tiger Hunt ■ 2011

10 x 11 inches (25.4 x 27.9 cm)
Porcelain; single fired, cone 10, black oxide and underglaze
inkjet print, colored underglazes, Japanese tissue paper
PHOTO BY KEN HODGE

CARLOS DYE
Into the Woods ■ 2006
12 x 15 x 2 inches (30.5 x 38.1 x 5.1 cm)
Stoneware clay; image transfer, stenciled with underglaze
relief, multiple fired, cones 01-08, underglaze brushwork
PHOTO BY SIERRA HAGBERG

85

BETSY KOPSHINA SCHULZ
The Sapphire Tower, San Diego, California ■ 2010
Each side of ten columns: 60 x 24 inches (152.4 x 61 cm)
White clay; multiple fired, cone 06-1, underglaze,
one-color screening onto wet clay
PHOTOS BY ARTIST AND INSU NUZZI

GREGORY ALIBERTI

P.J. McIntyre's Irish Pub ■ 2007

Tile; multiple fired, cone 04-1

PHOTOS BY WETZLER STUDIOS

MÓNICA GREZ
Vases ■ 2011
Tallest: 9 x 4 1/2 x 2 1/2 inches (22.9 x 11.4 x 6.4 cm)
Wheel-thrown stoneware; tissue-paper
transfer, glaze, electric fired, cone 9
PHOTO BY MARCELA GREZ BAUZÁ

BEATRÍZ HAMEL
Pot ■ 2011
4 x 5 x 3¹⁄₂ inches (10.2 x 12.7 x 8.9 cm)
Hand-built stoneware; tissue-paper transfer, macro-
crystalline glaze, matte glaze, electric fired, cone 9
PHOTO BY MARCELA GREZ BAUZÁ

JAMES SCHMOOCK
DEIDRE SCHMOOCK
Acer Palmatum ■ 2011
5 x 5¹⁄₂ x 3¹⁄₂ inches (12.7 x 14 x 8.9 cm)
Wheel-thrown and altered stoneware;
stenciled, electric fired, cone 6
PHOTO BY ARTISTS

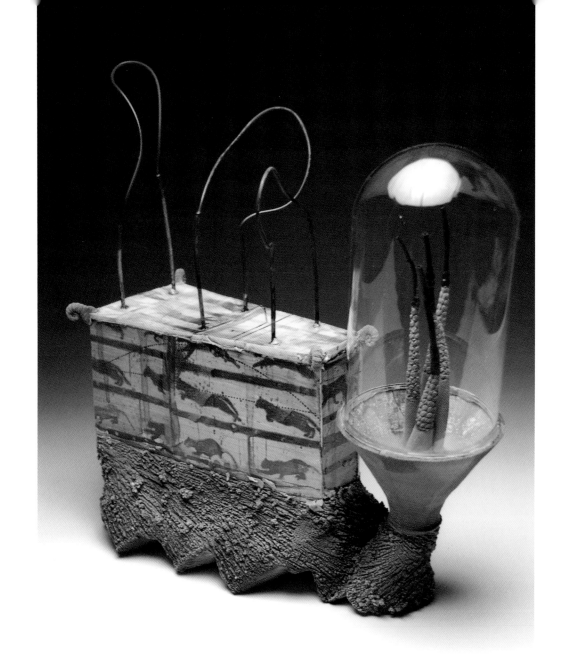

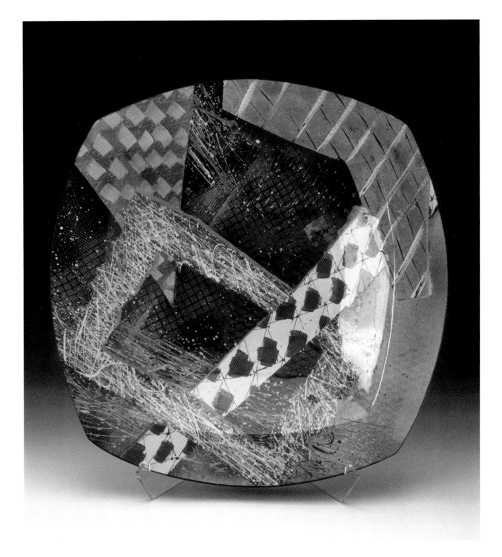

STEVE HOWELL
Square Platter ■ 1994

26 x 26 inches (66 x 66 cm)
Earthenware clay; multiple fired, cone 03-018,
images built up with underglazes in reverse on
plaster then transferred to earthenware slabs
PHOTO BY RANDALL SMITH

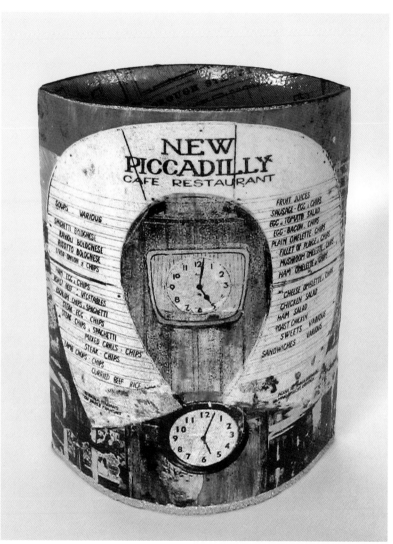

ANNABEL FARADAY
New Piccadilly Café ■ 2007
8 x 5¹⁄₂ x 4 inches (20.3 x 14 x 10.2 cm)
Stoneware crank; stenciled color slip, clear glaze
PHOTOS BY ARTIST

ISRAEL SHAWN DAVIS
Yunomi Series: Here's to the Birthday Boy Dreaming ■ 2011
5 x 3¹⁄₂ x 3¹⁄₂ inches (12.7 x 8.9 x 8.9 cm)
Slab-built red stoneware; wood fired, cone 10, porcelain slip, direct
screen-print on clay with underglaze, hand-painted color separations
PHOTO BY ARTIST

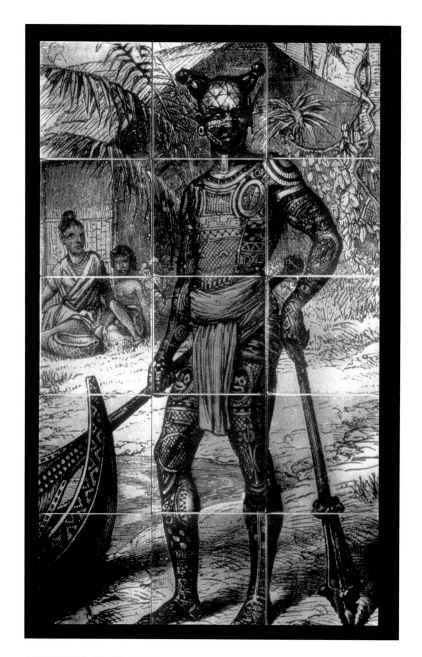

ANTHONY E. STELLACCIO
Essence ■ 2003
30 x 18 x ¼ inches (76.2 x 45.7 x 0.6 cm)
Earthenware clay; glaze, oxidation fired,
cone 04, underglaze screen-print
PHOTO BY DAN MEYERS

MARUTA MARIZA RAUDE
Bathroom Sink, Different Animals ■ 2010
5 7/8 x 16 15/16 x 21 5/8 inches (15 x 43 x 55 cm)
Factory-made stoneware, decals; onglaze painting
PHOTOS BY ARTIST

95

JIM GORDON JOHNSTONE
Oregon Coast ■ 2010
13 x 9 x 4½ inches (33 x 22.9 x 11.4 cm)
Slab-constructed stoneware,
laser decals; cone 6, stain, glaze
PHOTOS BY ARTIST

DIANA IRAGO
Graffiti 1 (Second Century A.D. Adriano's Empire) ■ 2009
16 x 21 inches (40.6 x 53.3 cm)
Earthenware clay, photocopies, laser decals, ceramic pigments;
image transfer to leather-hard clay, glazed, multiple fired in electric kiln
PHOTO BY LUCIA ANTONIETTI

97

BARBARA L. FREY
Offering #3 ■ 2010
9 x 14 x 16 inches (22.9 x 35.6 x 40.6 cm)
Hand-built porcelain; slips, glazes, cone 6,
newspaper-transfer printing with slips
PHOTO BY HARRISON EVANS

CLAYTON GEORGE BAILEY
Melted Hyperthermic Jug ■ 1994
25 x 24 x 25 inches (63.5 x 61 x 63.5 cm)
Stoneware; silk-screened, underglaze tissue transfer
PHOTO BY ARTIST

PHIL HARALAM
Eggshells ▪ 2011
48 x 24 x 24 inches (121.9 x 61 x 61 cm)
Porcelain; multiple-fired, cone 05-6,
underglaze, glaze, laser-decal transfer

STEVE ROYSTON BROWN
Moreau Archipelago ■ 2010
8 x 6 x 12 inches (20.3 x 15.2 x 30.5 cm)
Porcelain; fired, underglaze, multi-color
screen-printed, in-mold decoration
PHOTO BY ARTIST

GLORIA SINGER
Untitled ■ 2011
10½ x 13 x 3 inches (26.7 x 33 x 7.6 cm)
Hand-built white stoneware clay; oxidation fired, cone 6,
stamped with stain, stenciled with porcelain slip, carved
PHOTO BY ARTIST

TERRIE BANHAZL
It's Just Like Printing Money! ■ 2011

6 x 8 inches (15.2 x 20.3 cm)
Porcelain whiteware, china paint; laser-printer transfer
PHOTO BY SUSAN LEVY SCHALE

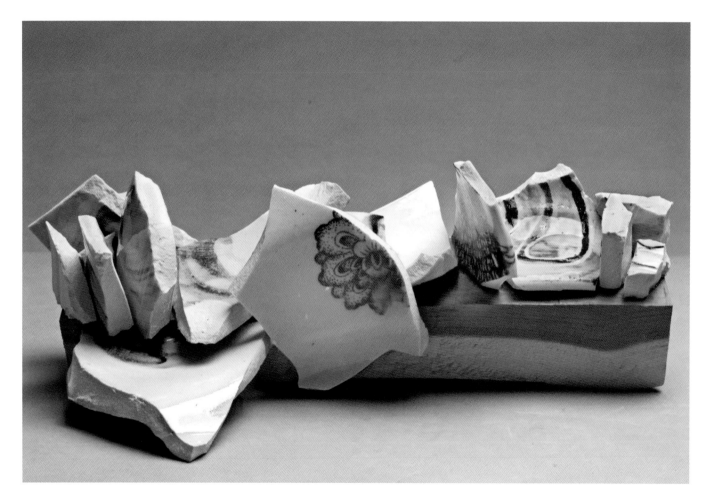

TERRY ADA DEBARDELABEN
Matrocliny: From the Mother—Shards ■ 2011
3 x 8 x 2 inches (7.6 x 20.3 x 12.4 cm)
Porcelain clay, decals, copperized water, oak; slip, cone 6
PHOTO BY JARVIS GRANT

KARL MCDADE
LESLEY BAKER
Amphora ■ 2007
14 x 21 x 14 inches (35.6 x 53.3 x 35.6 cm)
Cone 5 cobalt underglaze transfers,
clear glaze, overglaze decals
PHOTO BY ARTISTS

VALERIE ZIMANY
Chigiri-e (Radio Gold) ■ 2009
10 x 13 x 13 inches (25.4 x 33 x 33 cm)
Porcelain, decals, gold; multiple fired, cone 6,
cone 018, glaze, silk-screened, overglaze
PHOTOS BY ARTIST

LUBA SHARAPAN
Victorian Dystopia Mug ■ 2011
5 x 4½ x 3 inches (12.7 x 11.4 x 7.6 cm)
Porcelain clay, ceramic decals; multiple
fired, cone 018-6, colored slips
PHOTO BY ARTIST

107

MEL ROBSON
Precious Little ■ 2006
Each: 1 9/16 inches (4 cm) tall
Slip-cast porcelain, custom decals
PHOTO BY ARTIST

MELYNN ALLEN
Set of Three Mugs ■ 2011
Each: 4 1/2 x 3 x 3 1/2 inches (11.4 x 7.6 x 8.9 cm)
Wheel-thrown red stoneware, laser decals;
multiple fired, cone 6-04, multiple glazes
PHOTO BY ARTIST

KERI STRAKA
Cellular ■ 2011
7 x 12 x 14 inches (17.8 x 30.5 x 35.6 cm)
Porcelain clay; lithographic printing,
ceramic-stain washes, oxidation fired, cone 6
PHOTO BY ARTIST

MOLLIE BOSWORTH
Scattered Possibilities ■ 2011
2½ x 16 x 12 inches (6.4 x 40.6 x 30.5 cm)
Porcelain; multiple fired, cones 06 and 10,
laser-print decal slip, engobes, dry glazes
PHOTOS BY ARTIST

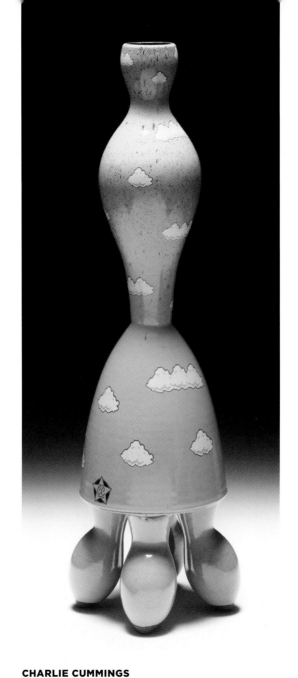

CHARLIE CUMMINGS
Stratospheric Vase ■ 2007
21½ x 5½ x 5½ inches (54.6 x 14 x 14 cm)
Thrown and slip-cast earthenware;
spot-color overglaze enamel decals
PHOTO BY ARTIST

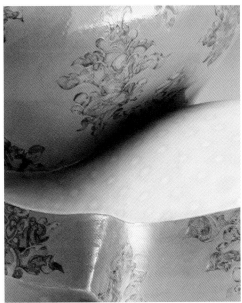

ERIN BETH FURIMSKY
Push ■ 2009
11 x 13 x 9 inches (27.9 x 33 x 22.9 cm)
Hand-built stoneware; underglazes,
stenciled, stamped, cone 04
PHOTOS BY TYLER LOTZ

113

RI VAN VEEN
Irezumi ■ 2011
15 x 12½ x 6½ inches (38.1 x 31.8 x 16.5 cm)
Raku clay; slab, tissue transfer,
clear satin glaze, fired, cone 03
PHOTO BY IAN HILL

AMY SANTOFERRARO
Philadelphia Upperware ■ 2009

13 x 9 x 7 inches (33 x 22.9 x 17.8 cm)
Slip-cast porcelain, decals, found materials
PHOTO BY ARTIST

MARIA ALEXA COHEN
Twilight Zone Marathon ■ 2011
25 x 14 ½ x 1 inches (63.5 x 36.8 x 2.5 cm)
White stoneware clay; screen-printed underglaze
PHOTO BY ARTIST

MAIJU ALTPERE-WOODHEAD
Soul's Garden ■ 2010
38⁹/₁₆ x 38⁹/₁₆ inches (97.9 x 97.9 cm)
Porcelain; fired, colored, monoprint, erosion
PHOTOS BY DEREK ROSS

STEPHANIE OSSER
Sketches of Renee and Her Piano Accompanist ■ 2011

3¹/₂ x 9 x 2¹/₂ inches (8.9 x 22.9 x 6.4 cm)
Porcelain; underglaze, glaze, screened,
carved, oxidation fired, cone 9
PHOTO BY TERESA LATTANZIO

119

SUZANNE SHARPE SIDEBOTTOM
Adventures in Art History ■ 2011
4 x 12 x 11 inches (10.2 x 30.5 x 27.9 cm)
Porcelain clay, rubber stamps created from drawn or digital images;
multiple fired, cone 04-5, underglaze, underglaze pencil, stamped
PHOTO BY ARTIST

JENNY HODGE
Paper Rhino ■ 2009
5⁹⁄₁₆ x 8 x 4 inches (14.1 x 20.3 x 10.2 cm)
Porcelain; single fired, cone 10, black oxide and
underglaze inkjet print, colored underglazes
PHOTO BY KEN HODGE

GEORGIA BRIGID SHEARMAN
Cutting Ties ■ 2011
15 x 10 inches (38.1 x 25.4 cm)
Earthenware clay, platinum luster, drawing by artist;
multiple fired, enamel transfer, press molded
PHOTO BY ARTIST

CHARLENE STALLARD
Printed Pitcher ■ 2011
9 1/2 x 6 x 5 inches (24.1 x 15.2 x 12.7 cm)
Semi-porcelain; cone 6, glaze, engobe, underglaze
PHOTO BY RORY MCDONALD

FACING PAGE
POLLY JOHNSON
Thank You Bear ■ 2010

9 x 7¹⁄₂ x 5¹⁄₂ inches (22.9 x 19.1 x 14 cm)
Porcelain, commercial greenware decal;
cone 6, hand-built and commercial-
mold assemblage, underglaze
PHOTO BY DIETER TAMSON

SIN-YING CASSANDRA HO
From the Made in the Postmodern Era Series: No. 4 ■ 2008

15¹⁄₂ x 11¹⁄₄ x 8¹⁄₂ inches (39.4 x 28.6 x 21.6 cm)
Porcelain clay, cobalt pigment, clear glaze, decal; fired twice,
cones 10 and 04, hand painted, terra sigillata, computer transfer
PHOTO BY ARTIST

KELLY ANN SCHNORR
Bric-a-Brac ■ 2010
66 x 120 x 3 inches (167.6 x 304.8 x 7.6 cm)
Post-consumer dishware; decals, cold finish
PHOTOS BY ARTIST

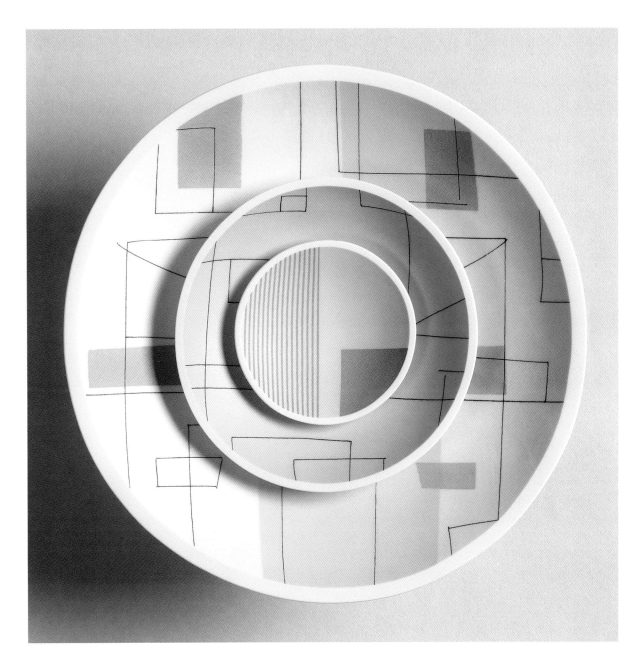

VICKY SHAW
Three Bowls ■ 2005

3 x 9 x 9 inches (7.6 x 22.9 x 22.9 cm)
Press-molded porcelain; fired, cone 8,
screen-printed underglaze color

SHARON VIRTUE
Three Queenie Tart Trivets ▪ 2011
Each: 6 x 7 x ½ inches (15.2 x 17.8 x 1.3 cm)
Earthenware clay; multiple fired, cones 1 and 07, printed
with texture and images, underglazes, translucent glazes
PHOTO BY ARTIST

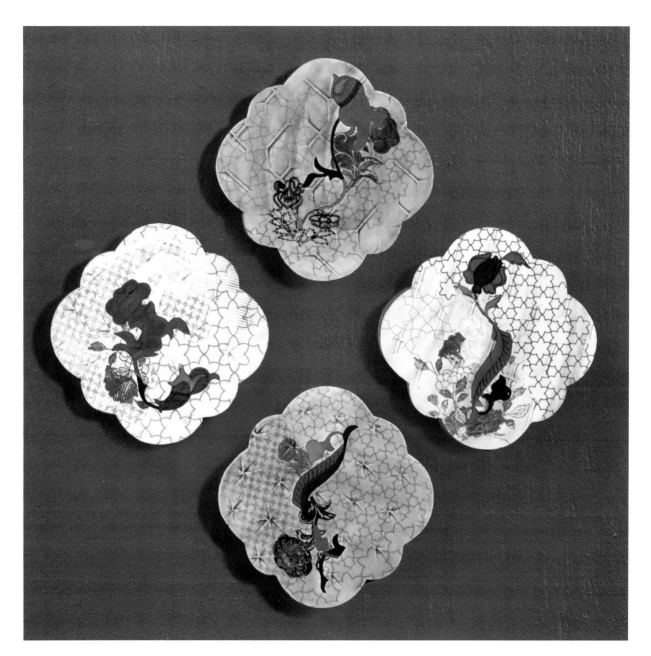

SANAM EMAMI
Trivets, Red-Brown Frame ■ 2011
24 x 24 x 1½ inches (61 x 61 x 3.8 cm)
Stoneware, paint; silk-screen transfers,
slip, electric fired, cone 6
PHOTO BY E.G. SCHEMPF

CAROL GENTITHES
Life's Little Pleasures ■ 2011
12 x 6 x 6 inches (30.5 x 15.2 x 15.2 cm)
Hand-thrown porcelain, decals;
multiple fired, cone 6-016, glaze
PHOTO BY ARTIST

THOMAS D. STOLLAR
Safety Second ■ 2010
7 x 8 x 7 inches (17.8 x 20.3 x 17.8 cm)
Slip-cast porcelain; cone 10,
screen-printed underglaze decals
PHOTO BY ARTIST

ELIZABETH VICTOR
Jungle Night ■ 2009
12 x 12 inches (30.5 x 30.5 cm)
Porcelain; cone 10, underglazes,
terra sigillata, monoprint
PHOTO BY MONICA RIPLEY

MARGARET TATTON-BROWN
Bee in Dappled Light ■ 2011

14 inches (35.6 cm) in diameter
Wheel-thrown stoneware; two glazes over
slips, stenciled, electric fired, cone 9
PHOTO BY STEPHEN BRAYNE

KARL MCDADE
LESLEY BAKER
Plate ■ 2007

20 x 20 x 4 inches (50.8 x 50.8 x 10.2 cm)
Cone 5, underglaze and overglaze transfers
PHOTO BY ARTISTS

500
prints on clay

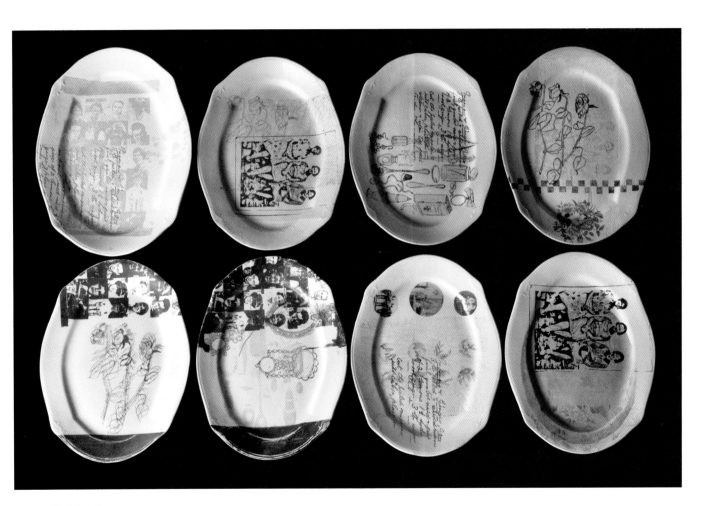

SALLY SZCZECH
Heirlooms ■ 2011

Each: 11½ x 15 inches (29.2 x 38.1 cm)
Slab-built porcelain, decals; screen-printed,
monoprint, cone 9, cone 04, electric fired
PHOTO BY SUSSIE AHLBURG

MOLLIE BOSWORTH
Magniflora ■ 2011
8 x 8 x 16 inches (20.3 x 20.3 x 40.6 cm)
Porcelain, laser-print decal; bisque fired, cone 10
PHOTO BY ARTIST

COURTNEY MURPHY
Nesting Set ■ 2011
8 x 15 x 15 inches (20.3 x 38.1 x 38.1 cm)
Terra cotta; cone 03, slip, glaze, terra sigillata
PHOTO BY ARTIST

VITA LENSKY-ZER
Why Not? ■ 2011
Each: 3⁷⁄₈ x 1⁷⁄₈ inches (9.8 x 4.8 cm)
Wheel-thrown earthenware;
cone 02, underglaze silk print
PHOTO BY ARTIST

CAMERON PAGE COVERT
Kabuki Edo Fireman ■ 2008
18 x 10 x 4 inches (45.7 x 25.4 x 10.2 cm)
Stoneware clay; low fired, cone 04, multiple fired, laser
transfer, underglaze, ceramic pencil, gloss overglaze
PHOTO BY ARTIST

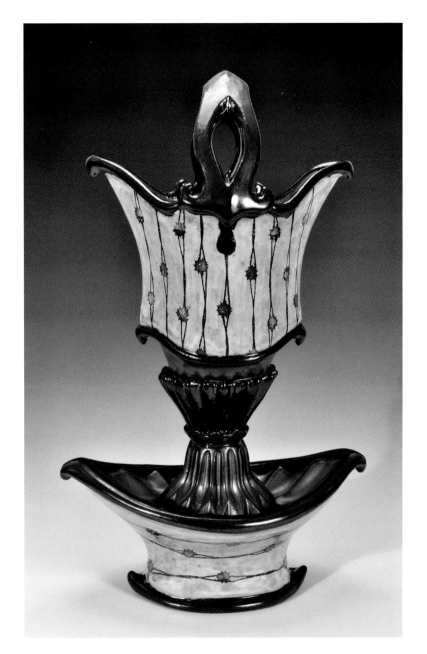

JEN GANDEE
Barbed Vessel ■ 2010
9 x 6 x 4 inches (22.9 x 15.2 x 10.2 cm)
Earthenware clay, laser decals; glaze
PHOTO BY ARTIST

MIRANDA HOWE
Fractured Pattern ■ 2009
9 x 27½ x 4½ inches (22.9 x 69.9 x 11.4 cm)
Stoneware; soda fired, cone 10, inlaid and
silkscreened underglaze, flashing slip, glaze
PHOTO BY ARTIST

CLARISSA MADGE REGAN
Boy in Story ■ 2009
4 ¹¹/₁₆ x 10 ⁵/₈ x 5 ⅛ inches (12 x 27 x 13 cm)
Porcelain paper clay, copper wash, laser decal; multiple fired,
cone 9-06, underglazes, glazes, silkscreened, stamped
PHOTO BY MICHEL BROUET

MATT L. CONLON
Untitled ■ 2011
4 1/2 x 3 3/4 x 1 1/2 inches (11.4 x 9.5 x 3.8 cm)
Porcelain; soda fired, cone 11, intaglio
PHOTO BY ARTIST

SONYA MCRAE
Coffee Pot with Cups ▧ 2009

Dimensions vary
Earthenware clay; fired, cone 04, screen-printed
underglaze, photocopy transfers and stamps, clear glaze

143

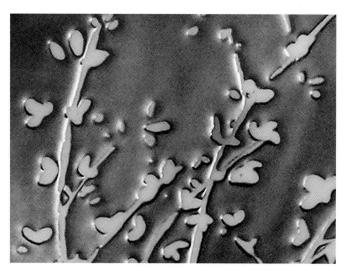

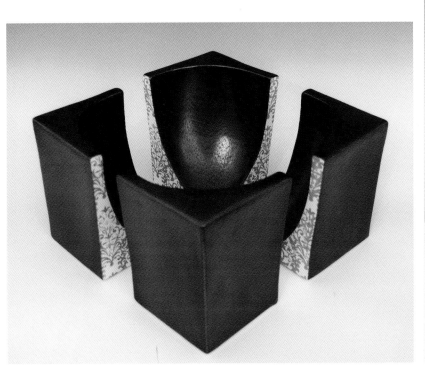

KAREN E. MURPHY
Untitled ■ 2011
6 x 9 x 9 inches (15.2 x 22.8 x 22.8 cm)
Slip-cast porcelain; fired, cone 6,
glaze, underglaze, silk-screened

CARLOS DYE
Cloud ■ 2006
13 x 15 x 2 inches (33 x 38.1 x 5.1 cm)
Stoneware clay; image transfer, stenciled with underglaze
relief, multiple fired, cones 01-08, underglaze brushwork
PHOTO BY SIERRA HAGBERG

JEFF IRWIN
Shooting Nature ■ 2011
29 x 41 inches (73.7 x 104.1 cm)
Earthenware tiles; laser-toner transfer,
glaze, sgraffito, cones 03 and 05
PHOTO BY ARTIST

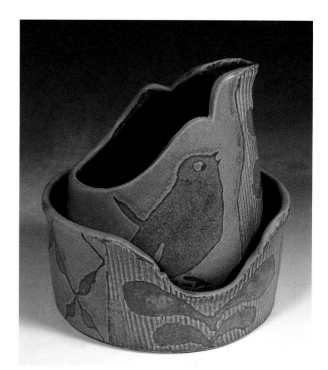

SHAWN O'CONNOR
Untitled ■ 2009
6 x 4½ x 4 inches (15.2 x 11.5 x 10.2 cm)
Porcelain; cone 10, black slip
silk-screened on freezer paper
and transferred to thrown surface

GLORIA SINGER
Creamer and Sugar Bowl ■ 2011
5 x 5 x 5 inches (12.7 x 12.7 x 12.7 cm)
Wheel-thrown, altered, and cut white
stoneware clay; oxidation fired, cone 6,
porcelain slip using paper stencils, wax resist

MARK DANITSCHEK
AMANDA DANITSCHEK
Blue ■ 2009
17 x 16 x 4 inches (43.2 x 40.6 x 10.2 cm)
Slab-built stoneware; electric fired, cone 5, underglaze
monotype print, matboard plate, direct-pressure press

JANET MARIE GADDY
Madonna of the Wind ■ 2009
6 x 6 inches (15.2 x 15.2 cm)
Porcelain clay, original graphic print; cone 6,
image transfer, acrylic varnish overlay
PHOTO BY TIMOTHY WINSPEAR MORAN

FACING PAGE
CHARLIE CUMMINGS
Returning to the Light ■ 2011
120 x 144 x 240 inches (304.8 x 365.8 x 609.6 cm)
Porcelain, earthenware clay; press molded,
four-color separation silk-screen, ceramic
monoprint, kiln glass cast, masked video
PHOTO BY RANDY BATISTA

SHARON BARTMANN
Home ■ 2011
3½ x 14 inches (8.9 x 35.6 cm)
Stoneware clay, original decals; multiple fired,
cones 04, 6, and 04, underglaze, glaze
PHOTOS BY PEGGY JO PETERSON

LAURA MARIE AULTMAN
Safety Plate ■ 2011

9½ inches (24.1 cm) in diameter
Wheel-thrown earthenware clay, laser
decal; multiple fired, cone 06-04, slips

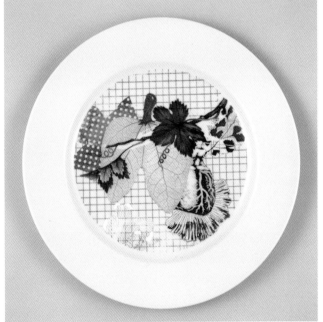

ANNA CALLUORI HOLCOMBE
Natura Vita I ■ 2009

11 inches (27.9 cm) in diameter
Commercial porcelain plate, vintage
and laser decals; cone 2, cone 018

JUSTIN ROTHSHANK
Sea Life Jar ■ 2011
9 x 8 x 8 inches (22.9 x 20.3 x 20.3 cm)
Earthenware clay, vintage decals, gold luster;
multiple fired, cone 04-015, laser-decal transfer

LESLEY BAKER
Fly on the Wall ■ 2009
18 x 26 x 4 inches (45.7 x 66 x 10.2 cm)
Stoneware clay, decals; multiple fired, cone 018-6,
underglaze, screen-printed, stenciled flocking
PHOTO BY ARTIST

GABRIELLE SIEGLINDE STURMAN
Lake Eacham Lightscape ■ 2011
Inset: 8 x 6 x ⅛ inches (20.3 x 15.2 x 0.3 cm)
Bone china, frame, electroluminescent
panel; cast, embossed
PHOTO BY SARAH SCRAGG

GERALDINE GANUN-OWENS
Sketchbook ■ 2010
8 x 16 x 5 inches (20.3 x 40.6 x 12.7 cm)
Mid-range porcelain clay; cone 04, underglaze,
underglaze pencil, glaze, cone 04/06, luster, cone 022
PHOTO BY ARTIST

JOHNTIMOTHY CHARLES PIZZUTO
Chasing the Shadow of Self ■ 2008
11 x 14 x 2 inches (27.9 x 35.6 x 5.1 cm)
Paper clay, acrylic; multiple screen
runs, drypoint collage, stamped
PHOTO BY ARTIST

PALUL PAUL RIDEOUT

Trinity ■ 2011

6¹⁄₂ x 5 inches (16.5 x 12.7 cm)
Grogged porcelain clay; woodcut plate stamped
into slab, bisque fired, cone 06; multiple underglazes
and glazes, intaglio, relief, high fired, cone 5
PHOTO BY ARTIST

159

SUSAN V. O'CONNOR
Untitled ■ 2011
1 x 4 x 9 inches (2.5 x 10.2 x 22.9 cm)
White stoneware, laser decal;
cone 06-6, slip, underglaze
PHOTO BY JENNY TURNER

KELLY ANN SCHNORR
Blue Lady Beers ■ 2011
Each: 6 x 4 x 4 inches (15.2 x 10.2 x 10.2 cm)
Stained porcelain, open-stock decals,
plastic; multiple fired, cone 10-018
PHOTO BY ARTIST

MARIA ESTHER BARBIERI
Towers of Babel ■ 2011
56 5/16 x 35 1/2 x 31 1/2 inches (143 x 90.2 x 80 cm)
Baskets, paper porcelain, decal;
cone 10, silk-screened, cone 015
PHOTO BY ANAXIMENES VERA

COLIN JOHN KLIMESH
Stemless Wine Glass ■ 2011
4 x 3 x 3 inches (10.2 x 7.6 x 7.6 cm)
Slip-cast white stoneware; cone 6, screen-printed overglaze decals, fired, cone 022

MOLLIE BOSWORTH
Bottlebrush Botanical ■ 2009
5 x 5½ x 5½ inches (12.7 x 14 x 14 cm)
Wheel-thrown porcelain, laser-print decal; fired, cone 10, polished

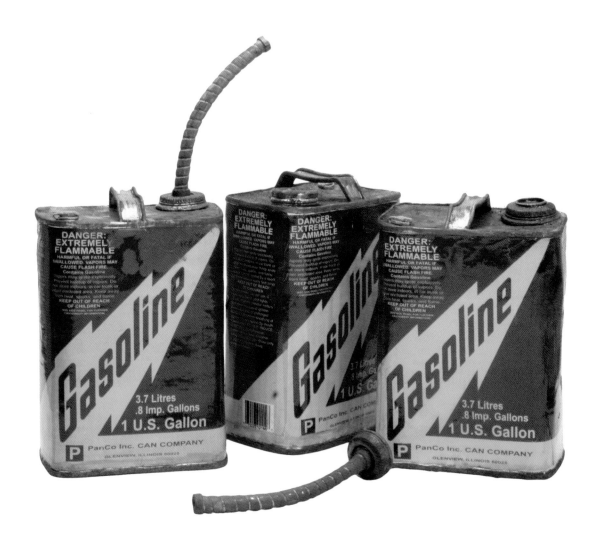

VIJAY V. PANIKER
Three Gas Cans ■ 2006

Each: 10 x 7 x 4 ³/₄ inches (25.4 x 17.8 x 12.1 cm)
Stoneware, decal; reduction fired, cone 10,
cone 018, lusters, iron oxides applied with china paint
PHOTO BY ANDREA M. ALLEN

ROBERT "BOOMER" MOORE
Non-Potable ■ 2011
13 x 10 x 10 inches (33 x 25.4 x 25.4 cm)
Slip-cast white ware, decal transfer;
fired, cone 1, underglaze
PHOTO BY BRETT KERN

SANAM EMAMI
Tulip Vases, Yellow Frame ■ 2009
16 x 34 x 12 inches (40.6 x 86.4 x 30.5 cm)
Porcelain, flowers, paint; electric fired,
cone 6, silk-screen transfers
PHOTO BY E.G. SCHEMPF

TALI COHEN-FLANTZ
In Memory I: Wall Installation ■ 2010

Each: 5½ x 5¼ x 3 inches (14 x 13.3 x 7.6 cm)
Slip-cast porcelain, decals, spices; wax resist,
sgraffito, clear glaze, fired, cone 9, cone 017
PHOTOS BY ARTIST

167

NANCY CREECH
Farm Dress ■ 2011
11¼ x 7¼ x 2¼ inches (28.6 x 18.4 x 5.7 cm)
Porcelain clay, mason stains; multiple fired,
cone 06-5, silk-screened with stained slip
PHOTO BY ARTIST

MATT LONG
Frying Pan ■ 2010
26½ x 18 x 3½ inches (67.3 x 45.7 x 8.9 cm)
Stoneware clay, mild steel; wood
fired, slips, glazes, stenciled
PHOTO BY ARTIST

169

ADAM PAULEK
Two Soup Bowls ■ 2011
Each: 3½ x 7 inches (8.9 x 17.8 cm)
Mid-range china clay, laser-transfer
decal; cones 5 and 05
PHOTO BY ARTIST

LANI MARIE SHAPTON
KEITH CARTER
~~Collection #2~~ ■ 2011

Each: 9 x 5 x 4 inches (22.9 x 12.7 x 10.2 cm)
High-fire slip-cast porcelain; black
underglaze pencil, clear glaze, cold finish

171

RHONDA UPPINGTON
Untitled ■ 2011

Left: 4 ¹/₂ x 3 ³/₄ x 3 ³/₄ inches (11.4 x 9.5 x 9.5 cm)
Right: 3 ³/₄ x 3 ¹/₄ x 3 ¹/₄ inches (9.5 x 8.2 x 8.2 cm)
Low-fire white clay; multiple fired, cone 05-04,
underglaze, clear glaze, collagraph print
PHOTO BY ARTIST

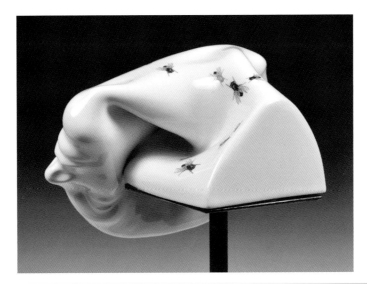

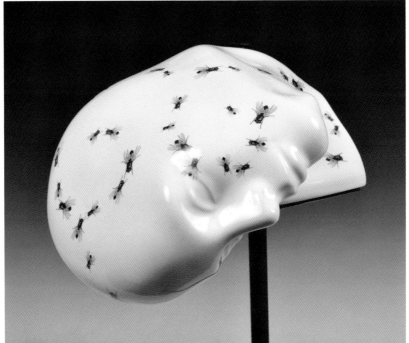

IVAN ALBREHT
Deflated Souvenir ■ 2009

6 x 9 x 8 inches (15.2 x 22.9 x 20.3 cm)
Porcelain; multiple fired, cone 4, cone 017, ceramic
decals printed from photopolymer plate
PHOTOS BY ARTIST

MICHAEL C. HOFFMAN
Westbound on M-211 ■ 2009
3¼ x 6½ x 6½ inches (8.3 x 16.5 x 16.5 cm)
Wheel-thrown clay, laser-printer decals; cone 5,
multiple fired, cone 6-06, cone 6, commercial glaze
PHOTO BY ARTIST

ULRIKA JARL
Globalization—Willow Pattern Reinterpreted ▪ 2010

10 inches (25.4 cm) in diameter
Second-hand porcelain plate, hand drawn,
digitally printed ceramic decal
PHOTO BY MARK HAWDON

175

KIP O'KRONGLY
Turbine Tumblers ■ 2010
Each: 7 x 2¼ x 2¼ inches (17.8 x 5.7 x 5.7 cm)
Wheel-thrown earthenware clay; underglaze,
single fired, cone 04, slips, stenciled, terra sigillata
PHOTO BY ARTIST

SANDRA TORRES
Tractor Set ■ 2011

Each cup: 3 1/4 x 3 inches (8.3 x 7.6 cm)
Slip-cast porcelain; multiple fired, cone 06-6,
soluble salts, cone 6 glaze, image transfer via paper
PHOTO BY ARTIST

RAIN HARRIS
Tangerine ■ 2009
12 x 10 x 4 inches (30.5 x 25.4 x 10.2 cm)
Slip-cast and altered porcelain, vintage decals;
cone 6, multiple fired, cone 6-018, glaze
PHOTO BY DOUG WEISSMAN

JILL OBERMAN
Bloom ■ 2010
18 x 24 x 3 inches (45.7 x 61 x 7.6 cm)
Porcelain clay; reduction fired, cone 9/10, stencil drawing
transfer on bisqueware, painted with wax resist, glazed, fired
PHOTO BY ARTIST

179

MARY ENG
Untitled Vase ■ 2011
8 x 3½ x 3½ inches (20.3 x 8.9 x 8.9 cm)
Stoneware; cone 6, slip, stenciled,
pressed through lace, clear glaze
PHOTO BY MONICA RIPLEY

CINDY HOSKISSON
Untitled ■ 2011
13 x 5 inches (33 x 12.7 cm)
Raku fired, laser-cut stencils
PHOTO BY DON HOSKISSON

CLAIRE TIETJE
White-Crowned Sparrow Bottle with Stopper ■ 2010
8 x 5 x 2 inches (20.3 x 12.7 x 5.1 cm)
Slab-built porcelain; carved, cone 5 oxidation, digital-image transfer, underglaze, colored slip, clear glaze

181

MEGAN R. MITCHELL
Landscape Diptych ■ 2010
6 x 16 inches (15.2 x 40.6 cm)
Porcelain, wood; reduction fired, cone 8, intaglio
print with ceramic ink, silk-screened underglaze

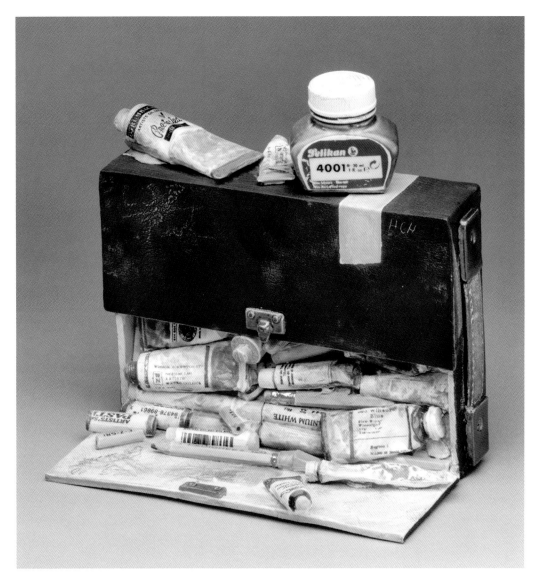

RICHARD BLAKE SHAW
Opened Black Paintbox Teapot ■ 2009
7½ x 8 x 5 inches (19.1 x 20.3 x 12.7 cm)
Glazed porcelain with overglaze decals
PHOTO BY ANTHONY CUÑHA

MARY ELIZABETH ENGEL
Ekphrasis ■ 2011
12 x 9½ x 4 inches (30.5 x 24.1 x 10.2 cm)
Earthenware clay, decals, gold luster;
multiple fired, cone 04-022
PHOTO BY CARLO NASISSE

500
prints on clay

CRISTINA DEL CASTILLO
Identities ■ 2009

47 1/4 x 23 5/8 inches (120 x 60 cm)
Earthenware clay; multiple fired, overglaze, one-color screening, stenciled on photopolymer plate
PHOTOS BY FERNANDO DEL CASTILLO

185

GARRY JOHN BISH
The Shadows Are as Important as the Light ■ 2008
5⅞ x 19¼ x 19¼ inches (15 x 49 x 49 cm)
Press-molded stoneware, decals, black
granite; multiple fired, silk-screened
PHOTO BY IAN HILL

PHYLLIS KLODA
Pampered Freak: Cha Cha Ahhh ■ 2010
5 x 8 x 7 inches (12.7 x 20.3 x 17.8 cm)
Slip-cast and hand-built white earthenware,
decals, luster, china paint; glaze

KALA STEIN
Presenting: Balance ■ 2011

6½ x 5¼ x ¾ inches (16.5 x 13.3 x 1.9 cm)
Slip-cast porcelain; cone 4, multiple
fired in oxidation, laser-decal transfer
PHOTO BY ARTIST

ALI SOBEL-READ
Hemispheres: Northern Crane, Southern Cross ■ 2011
13 ³/₄ x 8 ¹/₂ inches (34.9 x 21.6 cm)
Stoneware clay; underglaze, glaze, cone 05,
stenciled, multi-layered photo silk-screened prints

KAREN E. MURPHY
Untitled ■ 2011
17 x 9 x 8 inches (43.1 x 22.8 x 20.3 cm)
Slip-cast porcelain; fired, cone 6,
glaze, underglaze, silk-screened
PHOTOS BY ARTIST

TERRY ADA DEBARDELABEN
Matrocliny: From the Mother—Cheaper by the Dozen ■ 2011
Each: 6 x 2 x 1 inches (15.2 x 5.1 x 2.5 cm)
Porcelain clay, stoneware clay, decals; cone 6, clear glaze
PHOTO BY JARVIS GRANT

BARBARA L. FREY
Offering #5 ■ 2010
9 x 14 x 12 inches (22.9 x 35.6 x 30.5 cm)
Hand-built porcelain; slips, glazes, cone 6,
newspaper-transfer printing with slips
PHOTO BY HARRISON EVANS

MICHAEL T. SCHMIDT
Kendall Oil Can and Cups ■ 2010
15 x 11 x 18 inches (38.1 x 27.9 x 45.7 cm)
Porcelain, nichrome wire; soda fired, cone 10,
laser-print transfer, cast plaster base
PHOTO BY ARTIST

VIJAY V. PANIKER
Three Mini-Cans ■ 2006

Each: 6 3/4 x 3 x 1 3/4 inches (17.1 x 7.6 x 4.4 cm)
Stoneware, decal; reduction fired, cone 10, cone
018, lusters, iron oxides applied with china paint
PHOTO BY ANDREA M. ALLEN

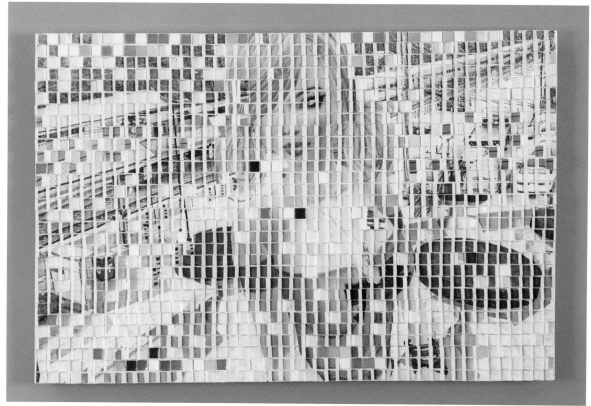

MEGUMI NAITOH
July 14, 2009 ■ 2009
19¹⁄₂ x 30³⁄₄ x 2 inches (49.5 x 78.1 x 5.1 cm)
Low-fired earthenware tiles; underglaze,
four-color separation screening
PHOTOS BY ARTIST

DIANE EMERSON
Resting Tree ■ 2010
5½ x 5½ inches (14 x 14 cm)
Slab-rolled clay, cedar sprigs; linocut embossing,
carved grout line, oxide, glaze, electric fired, cone 05
PHOTO BY JOHN CARLANO

JUAN GRANADOS
Ellas Dos (Including Two) ■ 2010
15 x 8 x 5 inches (38.1 x 20.3 x 12.7 cm)
Earthenware clay; glaze, raku fired,
cone 05, image transfer
PHOTO BY ARTIST

The quote on the artwork reads:

"Patriotism is a kind of religion; it is the egg from which wars are hatched..........."
—Guy de Maupassant

NANCY D. HERMAN
Untitled ■ 2011
6½ x 6½ x 4 inches (16.5 x 16.5 x 10.2 cm)
Porcelain, laser decal; underglaze, cone 05, cast
PHOTO BY TIM BARNWELL

ANA GÓMEZ
Buen Provecho (Bon Appetit) ■ 2009
11½ x 15 inches (29.2 x 38.1 cm)
Stoneware, decal; multiple fired, cone 6-015, glaze
PHOTO BY LUIS TIERRASNEGRAS

KARL MCDADE
Feeding the Bull ■ 2008

26 x 26 x 4 inches (66 x 66 x 10.2 cm)
Terra cotta; wood fired, cone 1,
underglaze screen-printed transfers
PHOTO BY ARTIST

201

MICHAEL T. SCHMIDT
Gulf and BP Teabowls ■ 2010
8 x 16 x 6 inches (20.3 x 40.6 x 15.2 cm)
Porcelain; soda fired, cone 10,
laser-print transfer, cast plaster base
PHOTO BY ARTIST

LORETTA LANGUET
Crackle Cups ■ 2009

Each: 7 1/2 x 7 1/2 x 7 1/2 inches (19.1 x 19.1 x 19.1 cm)
Stoneware, artist-designed stencils and
drawing; salt fired, wax resist, crackle slip
PHOTO BY ARTIST

MARY ELIZABETH ENGEL
Cat on Top of the World ■ 2011
8½ x 11 inches (21.6 x 27.9 cm)
Earthenware clay, decals, gold luster;
multiple fired, cone 04-022
PHOTO BY CARLO NASISSE

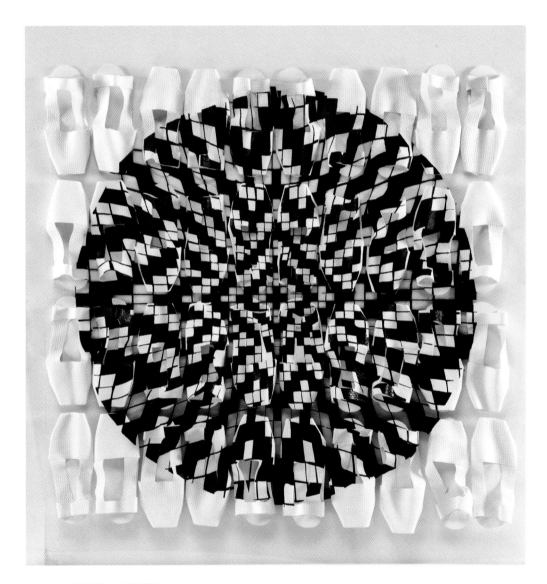

MARIA ESTHER BARBIERI
Jorop Art ■ 2009
33½ x 35½ x 2 inches (85.1 x 90.2 x 5.1 cm)
Slab-built porcelain, decal; cone
10, silk-screened, cone 016
PHOTO BY ANAXIMENES VERA

205

LAURA MCKIBBON
Untitled ■ 2011

Dimensions vary
Hand-built earthenware; press
molds of photopolymer plates
PHOTO BY ARTIST

HAYNE BAYLESS
Cream and Sugar Set ■ 2010

Left: 7 x 4 x 3 inches (17.8 x 10.2 x 7.6 cm)
Right: 7 x 8 x 3 inches (17.8 x 20.3 x 7.6 cm)
Hand-built white stoneware; reduction fired,
cone 10, slip stenciled, printed onto damp slab
PHOTO BY ARTIST

207

SHIN-YEON JEON
Waiting Too Long ■ 2011
16 x 13¼ inches (40.6 x 33.7 cm)
Terra-cotta clay; fired, cone 03,
underglaze, monoprint, clear glaze
PHOTO BY ARTIST

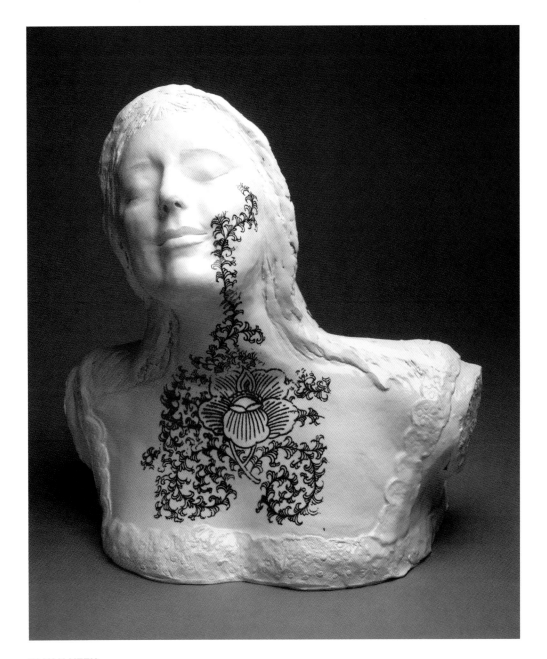

RI VAN VEEN
Back to Nature ■ 2011
16 x 16 x 11 inches (40.6 x 40.6 x 27.9 cm)
Hand-built raku clay; terra sigillata, tissue
transfer, clear satin glaze, fired, cone 03
PHOTO BY IAN HILL

MARC J. BARR
Tea Set 150 ■ 2009

Teapot: 10 x 6 x 4 inches (25.4 x 15.2 x 10.2 cm)
Stoneware clay; cone 5, multiple-color
screening, photopolymer relief
PHOTO BY ARTIST

MARTIN MÖHWALD
Teapot and Two Bowls ■ 2011

Dimensions vary
Stoneware; multiple fired, cone 06-6,
underglaze porcelain slip
PHOTO BY REINHARD HENTZE

DANIEL LISTWAN
Specimen II Contained ■ 2011
36 x 14 x 14 inches (91.4 x 35.6 x 35.6 cm)
Stoneware, glaze, luster, acrylic, glass, plastic
tubing, cold decal from original drawing
PHOTOS BY ARTIST

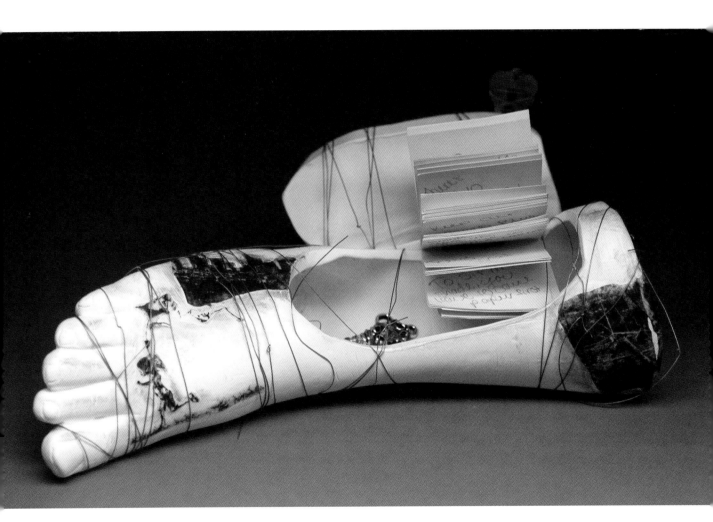

BAMBI FREEMAN
Sustainability ■ 2011
3 x 12 x 7 inches (7.6 x 30.5 x 17.8 cm)
Domestic porcelain clay, decals, waxed linen thread, linear paper,
bronze wire; fired, cone 06, gel transfer, Coptic-style book binding
PHOTO BY SHELDON GANSTROM

STEPHANIE NICOLE MARTIN
Untitled ■ 2011
Each: 7½ x 4 x 3 inches (19.1 x 10.2 x 7.6 cm)
Earthenware, laser decals;
cone 04, underglaze, slips
PHOTO BY JUAN VILLA

WENDY KERSHAW
She Wore Her Favorite Shirt ■ 2011
15 9/16 x 6 9/16 inches (39.5 x 16.7 cm)
Porcelain, ceramic decals;
cones 06, 6, and 014, underglaze
PHOTO BY ARTIST

JULIE GUYOT
Corn Sisters ■ 2011
Each: 15 x 5 inches (38.1 x 12.7 cm)
Earthenware clay, laser decals; multiple fired,
cone 010-04, underglaze, silk-screened slip transfers
PHOTO BY ARTIST

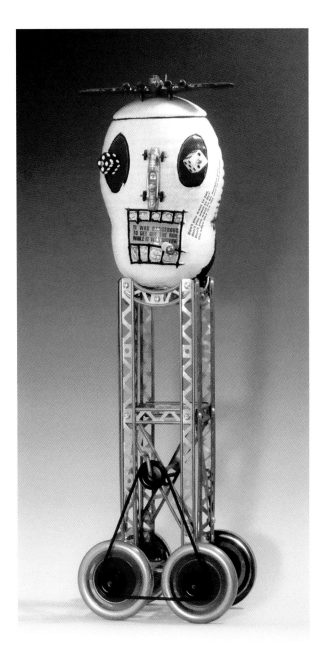

TOM BARTEL
Leopard Bust ■ 2010
24 x 12 x 10 inches (61 x 30.5 x 25.4 cm)
Earthenware; underglaze,
vitreous slip, screen-printed
PHOTO BY STEVE PASYT

DERIK VAN BEERS
It Wasn't Safe ■ 2011
21 x 7 x 6½ inches (53.3 x 17.8 x 16.5 cm)
Stoneware clay, paint, ceramic decals, metal shelf,
found objects; multiple fired, cone 05 and 017, glaze
PHOTO BY ARTIST

BRIAN SARAMA
Untitled 2 ■ 2011
5 x 14 x 8 inches (12.7 x 35.6 x 20.3 cm)
Porcelain, concrete; cone 7,
silk-screened, spray painted
PHOTO BY ARTIST

HAYNE BAYLESS
Teapot with Hinged Lid ■ 2011
9 x 12 x 4 inches (22.9 x 30.5 x 10.2 cm)
Hand-built stoneware; reduction fired, cone 10,
slip stenciled, printed onto damp slab, copper matte glaze
PHOTO BY ARTIST

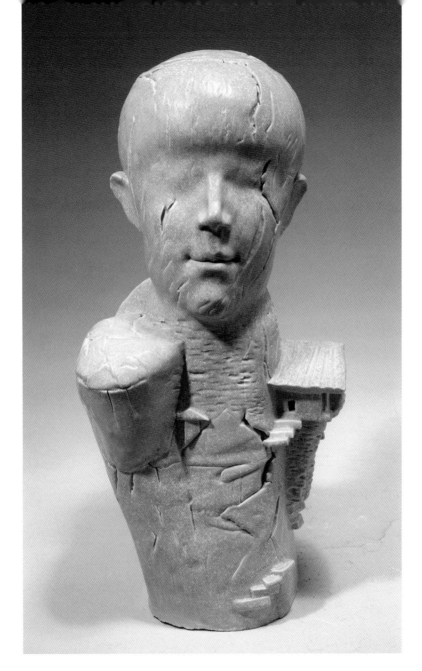

HONGWEI LI
Analogue #1 ■ 2006
18 x 10 x 9 inches (45.7 x 25.4 x 22.9 cm)
Porcelain clay; oxidation fired, cone 10, celadon
PHOTO BY ARTIST

MEREDITH HOST
Dot Dot Dash Tumblers ■ 2011

Each: 5¹⁄₂ x 3¹⁄₄ x 3¹⁄₄ inches (14 x 8.3 x 8.3 cm)
Porcelain, iron-oxide decals; multiple fired, cone 6-04,
underglaze, Thermofax screen-printing, stenciled
PHOTO BY ARTIST

BETTINA BAUMANN
Mutual Influences ■ 2009
11¹³/₁₆ x 35⁷/₁₆ x 13¹³/₁₆ inches (30 x 90 x 35.1 cm)
Stoneware clay, decal made by artist; multiple
fired, Orton cones 07, 7, 02, and 16, underglaze,
photographed, computer manipulated, transferred
PHOTO BY ARTIST

223

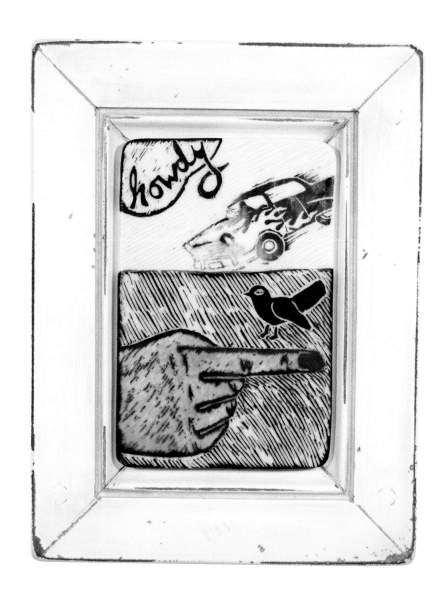

KATHY KING
Howdy ■ 2010
8 x 6¼ inches (20.3 x 15.9 cm)
Mid-range porcelain, wood;
screening, sgraffito, glaze, cone 6
PHOTO BY TERESA LATTANZIO PHOTOGRAPHY

JUAN GRANADOS
Otro Reflejo (Another Reflection) ■ 2010
16 1/2 x 8 x 5 inches (41.9 x 20.3 x 12.7 cm)
Earthenware clay; glaze, raku fired, cone 05, image transfer
PHOTO BY ARTIST

225

VALERIE ZIMANY
Chigiri-e (Kimono Blue) ■ 2010
13 x 15 x 15 inches (33 x 38.1 x 38.1 cm)
Porcelain; multiple fired, cone 6, cone 018, glaze, original
silk-screen overglaze decals, vintage commercial decals, gold
PHOTO BY ARTIST

MEL ROBSON
Fortitude (7) ■ 2009
4 x 2 inches (10.2 x 5.1 cm)
Slip-cast porcelain, custom decals
PHOTO BY ARTIST

MELYNN ALLEN
Poetry Bowl ■ 2011
3¹⁄₂ x 7 x 9 inches (8.9 x 17.8 x 22.9 cm)
Slip-cast buff stoneware, laser decals;
multiple fired, cone 6-04, multiple glazes
PHOTO BY ARTIST

SIGRID K. ZAHNER

Inconspicuous Consumption ■ 2011

12 x 20 x 5 inches (30.5 x 50.8 x 12.7 cm)

White earthenware clay; screen-printed, slip cast,
molded, underglazes and clear glaze, fired, cone 04

PHOTO BY WILBUR MONTGOMERY

MARIANA BAQUERO
Red and Yellow Pitcher and Cups ■ 2011

Dimensions vary
Wheel-thrown and altered porcelain, underglaze decals, custom-made laser-toner decals; multiple fired in oxidation, cone 05-6
PHOTO BY ARTIST

229

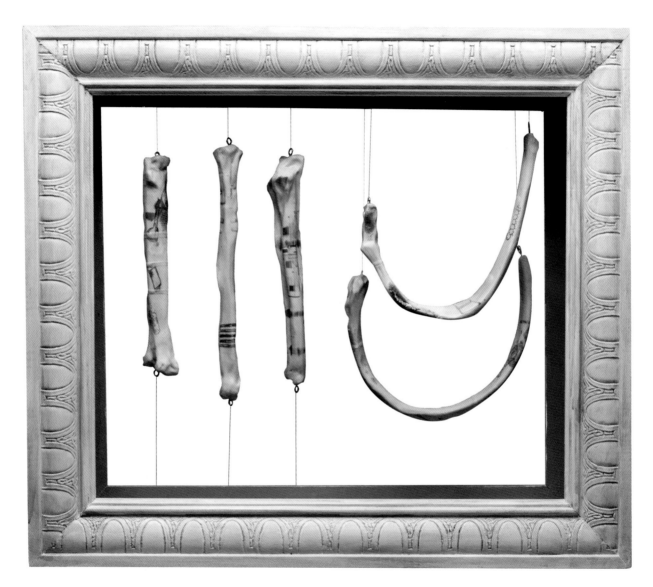

SARA ALLEN
Family Portrait Series: The South ■ 2009
20 x 24 x 5 inches (50.8 x 61 x 12.7 cm)
Soda-fired porcelain, photo decals, wooden frame; mixed
media, multiple fired, cone 04-6, inlaid engobe, glaze stencil
PHOTO BY ARTIST

500
prints on clay

CALDER KAMIN
Cardinalis cardinalis ■ 2008
8 x 16 x 6 inches (20.3 x 40.6 x 15.2 cm)
White earthenware, found drawer, string;
casting slip, cone 04, monoprint underglaze
PHOTO BY JEFF BRUCE

231

BARBARA HUMPAGE
Who Pleasure Gives Shall Joy Receive ■ 2011

15 inches (38.1 cm) in diameter
Earthenware clay; cone 04, colored slips and
glazes, direct screen-print on clay, sprigs
PHOTO BY DENNIS GORDON

SHAY AMBER
Trilogy of Celestial Beings I ■ 2010
13½ inches (34.3 cm) in diameter
Low-fire earthenware clay and wood; multiple fired,
stamped, china-paint and gold-luster image transfers
PHOTO BY ARTIST

233

MARIA INES VARELA
Diptych 1: El Observador ◾ 2010
Each section: 10 ⅝ x 10 ⅝ x 2 ¾ inches (27 x 27 x 7 cm)
Hand-built stoneware; pigments, engobes, electric fired, cone 8
PHOTO BY ALEJANDRO GALVEZ

KERRY JAMESON
The Figure ■ 2007
24 x 18 x 9 inches (61 x 45.7 x 22.9 cm)
Clay, found objects, earthenware;
multiple fired, silk-screen on clay
PHOTO BY ARTIST

LILIANNE MILGROM
Ruins of Mutanabi ■ 2008
7 x 11 inches (17.8 x 27.9 cm)
Porcelain; fired, smoked, wintergreen-
oil transfer from photocopy
PHOTO BY ARTIST

MARNEY ELIZABETH MCDIARMID
Untitled ■ 2009

8 x 7 x 7 inches (20.3 x 17.8 x 17.8 cm)
Hand-built porcelain; cone 6, relief,
stamped, photocopy transfer
PHOTO BY JEFFREY BARBEAU

237

SHALENE VALENZUELA
Scene #2: Noir Plate Series ■ 2011
7½ x 13 inches (19.1 x 33 cm)
Earthenware clay; cone 04, monoprinted
plate, underglaze, slip and pencil
PHOTO BY ARTIST

500
prints on clay

CHRIS RODI
Yank Series: Angela ■ 2011
9 ¾ x 11 ¾ inches (24.8 x 29.8 cm)
White stoneware; cone 5, underglaze,
four-color separation screened monoprint
PHOTO BY DOUG HETHERINGTON

239

DOUGLAS E. GRAY
Scandalous Tweets: Self Made ■ 2011
3 x 12 x 7 inches (7.6 x 30.5 x 17.8 cm)
White stoneware, decals; terra sigillata,
low-fire salt, paper saggar fired
PHOTO BY ARTIST

ERIN BETH FURIMSKY
Equate ■ 2009
18 x 8 x 6 inches (45.7 x 20.3 x 15.2 cm)
Hand-built stoneware, commercial decals;
underglaze, stenciled, multiple fired, cone 6-018
PHOTOS BY TYLER LOTZ

241

BRITTANY JO SCROGGINS
Green Wallpaper Bowl ■ 2011
2 ³⁄₄ x 6 x 6 inches (7 x 15.2 x 15.2 cm)
Red earthenware; cone 05, painted
slip, silk-screened slip, underglaze
PHOTO BY STEVE MANN

MEGAN R. MITCHELL
Diamond Platter ■ 2011
3 x 11 x 11 inches (7.6 x 27.9 x 27.9 cm)
Porcelain, decals; reduction fired, cone 9,
mold formed, slip transfers, underglaze, glaze
PHOTO BY ARTIST

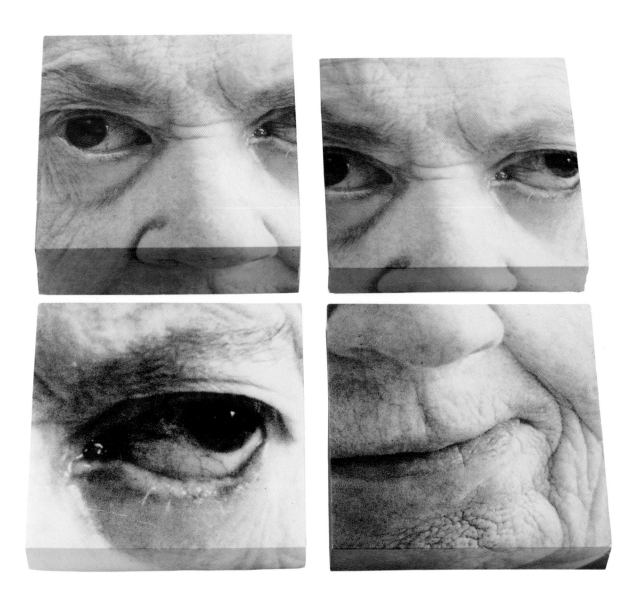

JEANNE OPGENHAFFEN
Darkness ■ 2010
Each: 7 7/8 x 7 7/8 inches (20 x 20 cm)
Stoneware, decals; glazed, screen-printed
PHOTO BY S. VAN HUL

STEVE GARCIA
Thirst ■ 2009

10 x 21 x 10 inches (25.4 x 53.3 x 25.4 cm)
Multiple fired, cast, on-glaze enamel prints
PHOTO BY ARTIST

SUN AE KIM
Teatotalism ■ 2011
Largest: 4 ¹¹/₁₆ x 10 ⁹/₁₆ x 10 ⁹/₁₆ inches (11.9 x 26.8 x 26.8 cm)
Bone china, enamel paint; multiple fired,
cones 8, 3, and 011, underglaze, digital-transfer print
PHOTOS BY ARTIST

FACING PAGE
FRIDA MÄLARBORN HOSHINO
*Bestrew Rose Petals on the Road
on Which We Wander* ■ 2006
39 ³/₈ x 39 ³/₈ inches (100 x 100 cm)
Installation of cast porcelain pieces with cobalt decals
PHOTO BY ANDERS OLOFSSON

MARIANA BAQUERO
Pitcher and Cups ■ 2011

Pitcher: 7 x 5½ inches (17.8 x 14 cm)
Wheel-thrown and altered porcelain, custom-made
laser-toner decals; multiple fired in oxidation,
cone 05-6, screen-printed underglaze
PHOTO BY ARTIST

AMY CHASE
Affliction ■ 2010
11 x 17 inches (27.9 x 43.2 cm)
Porcelain; reduction fired, cone 10,
flocking, silk-screened underglaze decals
PHOTO BY ARTIST

MEGAN R. MITCHELL
Teapot ■ 2008
4 x 8 x 8 inches (10.2 x 20.3 x 20.3 cm)
Hand-built porcelain; reduction fired, cone 10, mold
formed, silk-screened underglaze, stamped, glaze
PHOTO BY ARTIST

MARC J. BARR
Tea Set 196 ■ 2010
Assembled: 12 x 12 x 4 inches (30.5 x 30.5 x 10.2 cm)
Stoneware clay; cone 5, multiple-color
screening, photopolymer relief
PHOTO BY ARTIST

SIGRID K. ZAHNER
Upside Downside of Life ■ 2010
12 x 12 x 6 inches (30.5 x 30.5 x 15.2 cm)
Slip-cast and molded earthenware; screen-printed
underglazes, clear glazes, fired, cone 04
PHOTO BY ARTIST

251

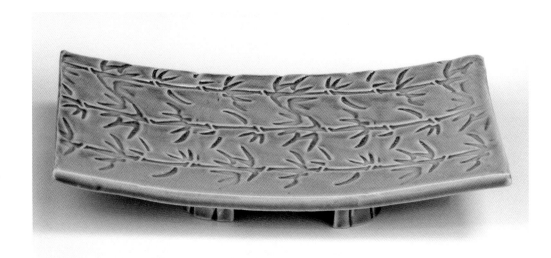

MIRANDA HOWE
Burnt Canyon ■ 2009
15 x 65 x 8½ inches (38.1 x 165.1 x 21.6 cm)
Stoneware; soda fired, cone 10, inlaid,
silk-screened underglaze, flashing slip, glaze
PHOTO BY ARTIST

JAMES SCHMOOCK
DEIDRE SCHMOOCK
Bamboo ■ 2011
2½ x 13½ x 7 inches (6.4 x 34.3 x 17.8 cm)
Slab-built, stamped, and hump-molded
stoneware; electric fired, cone 6
PHOTO BY ARTISTS

JEN GANDEE
Finger Bowl ■ 2008
10 x 6 x 6 inches (25.4 x 15.2 x 15.2 cm)
Hand-built earthenware; screen-
printed underglaze transfers
PHOTO BY ARTIST

KARL MCDADE
LESLEY BAKER
Kylix ■ 2007
14 x 20 x 16 inches (35.6 x 50.8 x 40.6 cm)
Cone 5, overglaze decals; flocking
PHOTOS BY ARTISTS

LAURA MCKIBBON
Finnish Flasks ■ 2011
Tallest: 7½ x 5 x 1 inches (19.1 x 12.7 x 2.5 cm)
Hand-built porcelain, photopolymer plates
PHOTOS BY ARTIST

BARB CLARK
Moonlit ■ 2011
8½ x 8 inches (21.6 x 20.3 cm)
Clay monotype from plaster slab; low fire, underglazes
PHOTO BY KELLY MCLENDON

257

CHRIS BLACKHURST
The Journey ■ 2009
31 x 84 x 5 inches (78.7 x 213.4 x 12.7 cm)
Commercial tile, acrylic, grout, medium-density fiberboard;
multiple fired, cone 06-04, underglaze, glaze, screen-printed
PHOTOS BY ARTIST

MEGUMI NAITOH
June 1, 2009 ■ 2009
19¹⁄₂ x 30¹⁄₂ x 2¹⁄₄ inches (49.5 x 77.5 x 5.7 cm)
Low-fire earthenware tiles; underglaze,
four-color separation screening
PHOTOS BY ARTIST

KEITH HERSHBERGER
Bird Plate ■ 2011

11 inches (27.9 cm) in diameter
Wood-fired stoneware; cone 10,
slip and flashing slip with paper stencils
PHOTO BY ARTIST

261

JIM LIEB
The Eye of the Storm ■ 2011
6 x 5 x 5 inches (15.2 x 12.7 x 12.7 cm)
Stoneware clay with porcelain slip;
fired, cone 6, silk-screened design
PHOTO BY STEVE O'TOOLE

FRANK JAMES FISHER
American Home ■ 2011
3³⁄₄ x 3¹⁄₂ x 3¹⁄₂ inches (9.5 x 8.9 x 8.9 cm)
Porcelain, impressed graphics from paint plates;
bisque, glazed, raku fired, combustibles
PHOTO BY ARTIST

RICHARD LAWSON
Naked Raku with Koi ■ 2011
18 x 8 inches (45.7 x 20.3 cm)
Laguna B-Mix with grog; transfers fired on greenware,
cone 06, raku fired with resist slip and glaze

EILEEN SACKMAN
Reliquary ■ 2010
21 x 12 x 12 inches (53.3 x 30.5 x 30.5 cm)
Cone 04 glaze, decal
PHOTOS BY ARTIST

BRENDAN OLDHAM
Some Kind of Nature ■ 2011
20 x 20 inches (50.8 x 50.8 cm)
Stoneware; silk-screened
underglaze, glaze, fired, cone 6
PHOTO BY ARTIST

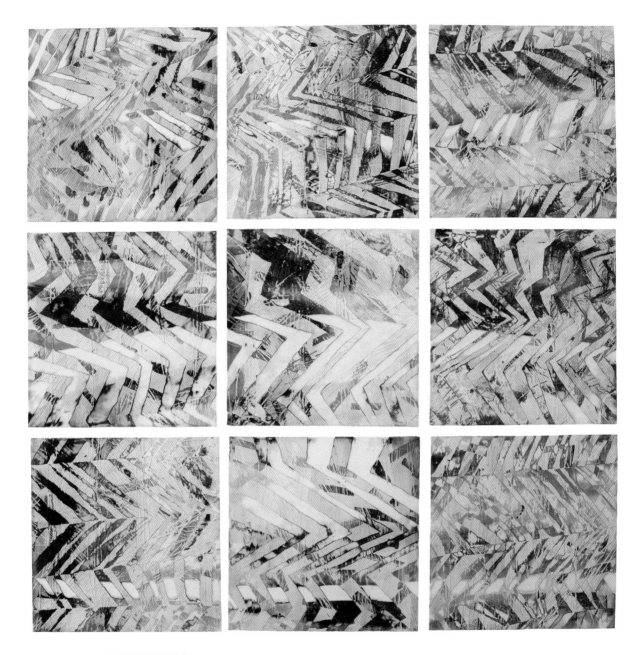

MAIJU ALTPERE-WOODHEAD
Echo ■ 2010
38 9/16 x 38 9/16 inches (97.9 x 97.9 cm)
Porcelain; fired, colored, monoprint, erosion
PHOTO BY DEREK ROSS

THOMAS R. LUCAS
Dorothy's Vase ■ 2010
8 x 6 x 6 inches (20.3 x 15.2 x 15.2 cm)
White stoneware clay; multiple fired,
cone 04-10, screen-printed
PHOTO BY ARTIST

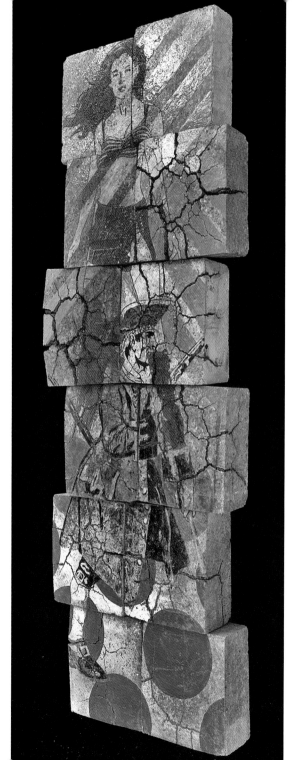

DANA CHILDS
Contrapposto ■ 2009
54 x 18 x 3 inches (137.2 x 45.7 x 7.6 cm)
Fire brick; multiple fired, cone 10-06, underglaze,
low-fire glaze, carbon-paper transfers, stenciled
PHOTO BY GORDON HUMPHRIES

S.U.B.P.A.R. (SYRACUSE URBAN BEAUTIFICATION PUBLIC ART RESISTANCE)
Phone Booth (Home) ■ 2011

Tile: 20 x 8 inches (50.8 x 20.3 cm)
Stoneware clay, phone booth; oxidation fired,
cone 04, colored slip, offset screen-printed transfer
PHOTOS BY ARTIST

WARREN MATHER
Telephone Pole ■ 2011

31 inches (78.7 cm) in diameter
Earthenware clay; glaze fired, cone 05, hand
colored with underglazes after single screen-print
PHOTO BY ARTIST

271

SUN AE KIM
Much-Loved Flat ■ 2011
12 x 7½ x 3½ inches (30.5 x 19.1 x 8.9 cm)
Bone china; multiple fired, cones 8, 3,
and 011, underglaze, screened transfer
PHOTO BY ARTIST

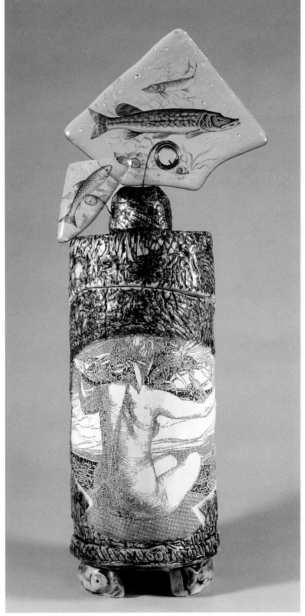

BETTY L. WILSON
Fresh Catch ■ 2011
16 x 6 x 6 inches (40.6 x 15.2 x 15.2 cm)
Stoneware clay, fused glass and wire with
decal; multiple fired, cone 04-6, copper
wash, clear glaze, laser-print transfer
PHOTOS BY DURGA GARCIA

273

LISA M. JOHNSON
Peacemaker Soup Tureen ■ 2009
9½ x 17½ x 10½ inches (24.1 x 44.5 x 26.7 cm)
Porcelain, copper, silver, decal; slip cast, fabricated,
multiple fired in electric kiln, cone 06-04
PHOTO BY MICHELLE GIVEN

500
prints on clay

JENI ANNE GARD
Purple Handspring Butter Dish ■ 2011

5 x 6 x 3 inches (12.7 x 15.2 x 7.6 cm)
Hand-built porcelain; cone 6, screen-printed
transfer with multiple underglazes
PHOTO BY FORREST GARD

ANJU KALSI
Untitled ■ 2007

6 x 9 inches (15.2 x 22.9 cm)
Wheel-thrown and altered
stoneware clay; underglaze decal
PHOTO BY ARTIST

All war is deception. Regard your soldiers as your children, and they will follow you into th deepest valleys; look on them as your own beloved sons, and they will stand by you even unto death."

We're not in Kansas anymore Toto

PAULA JEAN MORAN
War Games ■ 2011
16 x 16 inches (40.6 x 40.6 x 1.3 cm)
Stoneware; fired, cone 06-1, terra
sigillata, screen-printed, stenciled
PHOTO BY ARTIST

NICOLE THOSS
Kidnapping ■ 2010
13 ¹¹/₁₆ x 9 ¹³/₁₆ x 1 ⁷/₈ inches (34.8 x 24.9 x 4.8 cm)
Stoneware clay; engobe, lithography
print, transparent glaze, electric fired
PHOTO BY BAUMANN FOTOSTUDIO

TERRIE BANHAZL
Basket of Veggies ■ 2011

10 x 15 inches (25.4 x 38.1 cm)
Earthenware; bisque fired, glazes,
cone 06, laser-printer transfer
PHOTO BY SUSAN LEVY SCHALE

500
prints on clay

JULIETA CONSTANZA COSENTINO
Bajas Calorias ■ 2006
Each: 3 1/8 x 3 15/16 x 14 3/16 inches (8 x 10 x 36 cm)
Porcelain, earthenware clay; cone 6, underglaze transfer printing
PHOTOS BY FIDEL PEREZ

279

PHYLLIS KLODA
Pampered Freak: Wild Blue ■ 2010
8 x 7 x 7 inches (20.3 x 17.8 x 17.8 cm)
Slip-cast and hand-built white earthenware,
decals, luster, china paint; glaze
PHOTO BY ARTIST

MICHELLE H. HAMILTON
Darwin's Prose #3 ■ 2009
18 x 8 x 8 inches (45.7 x 20.3 x 20.3 cm)
Mid-fire white clay; cone 6, glaze, artist's
own photograph multilayered fired on decal
PHOTO BY JOSEPH GRUBER

SARAH KANDELL-GRITZMAKER
Scatter ■ 2010
28 x 24 x 6 inches (71.1 x 61 x 15.2 cm)
Porcelain, steel wire; photocopy
transfer prints, mason stain
PHOTOS BY DEREK BROWN

JEANNE OPGENHAFFEN
Absent-Present ■ 2002
49 3/16 x 49 3/16 inches (125 x 125 cm)
Stoneware, decals; glazed, three-
color separation, screen-printed
PHOTO BY S. VAN HUL

ANGELA WALFORD
Three Seasons in One Day, Wall Tile 1 ■ 2011
12 x 12 inches (30.5 x 30.5 x 0.6 cm)
Stoneware clay; cone 7, underglaze
decoration, slip, silk-screened, stenciled
PHOTO BY ARTIST

BEVERLY JAKUB AROH
Sunrise on the Road to Rand's Kiln ■ 2011
8³⁄₄ x 10¹⁄₂ x ¹⁄₄ inches (22.2 x 26.7 x 0.6 cm)
Stoneware clay; multiple fired in soda kiln, cone 06-10, underglaze
washes on lithograph and Thermofax screened images
PHOTO BY KATZ PHOTOGRAPHY

CHRIS RODI
Yank Series: Rita ■ 2011
13 ³/₄ x 17 ³/₄ x 1 inches (34.9 x 45.1 cm)
White stoneware; cone 5, underglaze,
four-color separation screened, monoprint
PHOTO BY DOUG HETHERINGTON

GARY ALLAN ERICKSON
Self-Portrait ■ 2011
21 x 21 inches (53.3 x 53.3 cm)
White earthenware; cone 05, underglaze decals
PHOTOS BY ARTIST

MOLLY I. BRAUHN
HERE/NOW ■ 2010
20 x 18 x 9 1/2 inches (50.8 x 45.7 x 24.1 cm)
Earthenware clay, decals; multiple fired,
cone 06-03, underglaze wash
PHOTO BY ARTIST

KAREN PATINKIN
Platter ■ 2010
15 inches (38.1 cm) in diameter
Wheel-thrown porcelain; gas fired, cone 10,
slips, glazes, screen-printed under clear glaze
PHOTO BY GUY NICOL

KIK SKAKEL WILLIAMS
Let's Play ■ 2010
7 inches (17.8 cm) in diameter
Stoneware clay, sepia decals, vintage colored decals;
color slip, multiple fired, cones 06, 6, 04, and 019, glaze
PHOTO BY ANDREW FLADEBOE

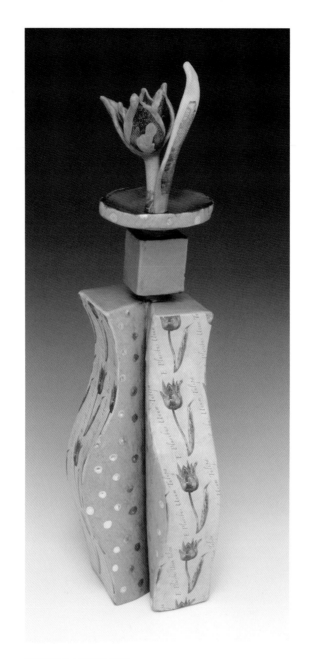

SANDRA LUEHRSEN
E-Pluribus Unum Tulipa ■ 2011
22 x 8 x 6 inches (55.9 x 20.3 x 15.2 cm)
Earthenware clay, artist-designed decals, metallic
luster; multiple fired, cone 019-03, glazes
PHOTO BY ARTIST

AMY SANTOFERRARO
Deer Plate ■ 2009
10 x 6 x 2 inches (25.4 x 15.2 x 5.1 cm)
Earthenware; fired, screen-printed
PHOTO BY ARTIST

RYTAS JAKIMAVIČIUS
Cup with Prayer ■ 2010
5 3/8 x 4 11/16 x 4 inches (13.7 x 11.9 x 10.2 cm)
Porcelain, decals; glazes, gas fired, cone 11,
cone 06, onglaze colors, cone 016
PHOTO BY ARTIST

RICHARD BLAKE SHAW
Canton Collection ■ 2009
6¹⁄₂ x 10¹⁄₂ x 10¹⁄₂ inches (16.5 x 26.7 x 26.7 cm)
Glazed porcelain with overglaze decals
PHOTO BY ANTHONY CUÑHA

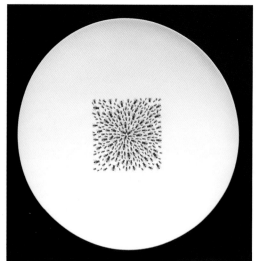

IVAN ALBREHT
Square ■ 2011

22 inches (55.9 cm) in diameter
Porcelain, ceramic decals; multiple fired,
glaze cone 1, cone 017, digital printing
PHOTOS BY ARTIST

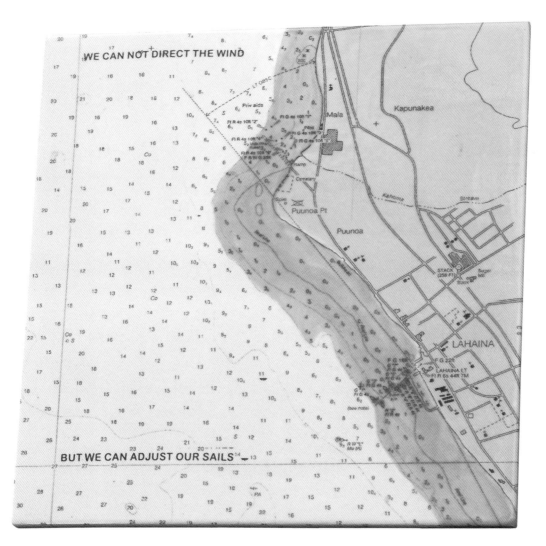

JUDITH BUSHNELL
THEO BUSHNELL

Any Port in a Storm Tile: Lahaina ■ 2010

8 x 8 inches (20.3 x 20.3 cm)
Hand built, slip cast, hand glazed, multiple
fired, cone 04-09, laser-printed decals

WARREN MATHER
Red Pine ■ 2010
36 inches (91.4 cm) in diameter
Earthenware clay; glaze fired, cone 05, hand
colored with underglazes after single screen-print
PHOTO BY ARTIST

PHIL HARALAM
It's Just Politics ■ 2011
12 x 11 x 11 inches (30.5 x 27.9 x 27.9 cm)
Porcelain, stoneware, china paint, laser decal; multiple fired,
cone 018-10, underglaze, glaze, soda fired, electric fired, cone 1
PHOTO BY ARTIST

NICOLE MARIE DEZELON
Letters Home ■ 2010

Each: 30 x 30 inches (76.2 x 76.2 cm)
Earthenware clay; oxides, multiple fired, low-fire
glazes, cone 05, toner transfers, cones 4-6
PHOTOS BY ARTIST

PENNY ERICSON
Building Blocks ■ 2011
15 x 12 x 4 ½ inches (38.1 x 30.5 x 11.4 cm)
Earthenware; fired, cone 02, viscosity print transfer
PHOTO BY ARTIST

FRANCES BROSNAN
Rochinha ■ 2011
7 x 5½ x 3½ inches (17.8 x 14 x 8.9 cm)
Porcelain clay, decals; multiple
fired, cone 05-7, underglaze
PHOTO BY DENIS DUNNE

LEMAN KALAY
Captivity ■ 2010
3 9/16 x 23 5/8 x 17 11/16 inches (9 x 60 x 45 cm)
Earthenware clay, wire; slip cast,
multiple fired, overglaze, laser printing
PHOTO BY GÖZDE YENIPAZARLI

GREG JAHN
NANCY HALTER
Treasure Stupa ■ 2011

5 x 4 x 4 inches (12.7 x 10.2 x 10.2 cm)
Porcelain; multiple fired, cones 10 and 017, high-fired shino,
silk-screened ceramic transfers of original drawings
PHOTO BY ARTISTS

NATHAN FALTER
Gas Can ■ 2011
18 x 10 x 10 inches (45.7 x 25.4 x 25.4 cm)
Wheel-thrown stoneware; slips, underglaze,
ash glaze, altered, assembled, stenciled
PHOTO BY ARTIST

JONES VON JONESTEIN
*From the von Jonestein Heritage
Foundation Commemorative Plate Series:
Dr. Reynard von Jonestein Singh* ■ 2011
11 x 16 x 3 inches (27.9 x 40.6 x 7.6 cm)
Porcelain, decals
PHOTO BY ARTIST

JUSTIN ROTHSHANK
Self-Portrait ■ 2011

14 inches (35.6 cm) in diameter
Earthenware clay, custom pancake decal;
multiple fired, cone 04-015, laser-decal transfer
PHOTO BY ARTIST

AARON MICHAEL CALVERT
Industrious Ant Teapot ■ 2009
9 x 6 x 5 inches (22.9 x 15.2 x 12.7 cm)
Thrown stoneware; reduction fired,
cone 10, glaze, stenciled, sandblasted
PHOTOS BY ARTIST

ANDREW GILLIATT
Mixed Tape Mug ■ 2011
4 x 5½ x 4 inches (10.2 x 14 x 10.2 cm)
Colored porcelain; glaze, laser
transfer, reduction fired, cone 10

NATALIE STEINMETZ
Express ■ 2008
18 x 15 x 3 inches (45.7 x 38.1 x 7.6 cm)
Wheel-thrown and hand-built earthenware
clay; cone 06, underglaze, silk-screened

SHAE BISHOP
Reflection ■ 2010
11 x 10 x 10 inches (27.9 x 25.4 x 25.4 cm)
White earthenware, terra cotta, copper wash; black
underglaze, glaze, monoprinted from plaster slab
PHOTO BY JIM WALKER

DAVID SCOTT BOGUS
The Optimist Luggage 9 ■ 2011
16 x 16 x 8 inches (40.6 x 40.6 x 20.3 cm)
Slip-cast white earthenware; multiple fired,
cone 06-018, luster, overglaze decal
PHOTO BY ARTIST

LISA SKOG
Untitled ■ 2011
13 x 11 inches (33 x 27.9 cm)
Raku clay, decals; stamped,
raku fired, encaustic media
PHOTO BY ARTIST

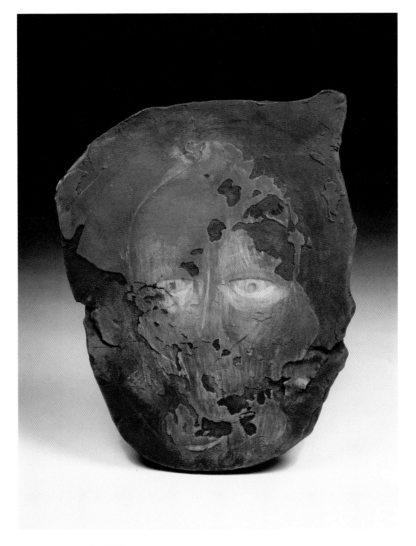

MIRIAM RAE-SILVER
Born of No Sound ■ 2011
13 x 9 inches (33 x 22.9 cm)
Earthenware clay; oxidation fired, monotype

PETER HOOGEBOOM
Holy Water (Necklace) ■ 2007
13 ³/₈ x 13 ³/₈ x ⁵/₁₆ inches (34 x 34 x 0.8 cm)
Stoneware, cotton, sealing wax, silver, decals
PHOTO BY FRANCES WILLEMSTIJN

RAIN HARRIS
Perennial ■ 2010
19 x 21 x 21 inches (48.3 x 53.3 x 53.3 cm)
Porcelain, iron-oxide decals, rhinestones;
multiple fired, cone 6-04, glaze, slip cast, altered
PHOTO BY DOUG WEISSMAN

TRUDY GOLLEY
Faux Banskia Vase ■ 2010
16½ x 7 x 3½ inches (41.9 x 17.8 x 8.9 cm)
Multi-fired porcelain, custom 24-karat gold
overglaze decals; slip cast, press molded
PHOTO BY PAUL LEATHERS

ANA GÓMEZ
Servicio Inglés (English Crockery Set) ■ 2009

Dimensions vary
Stoneware, decal, gold luster;
multiple fired, cones 6, 015, and 018, glaze
PHOTO BY LUIS TIERRASNEGRAS

317

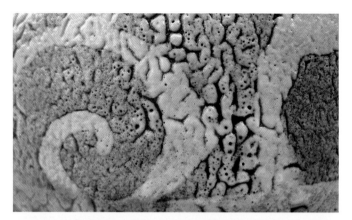

ZYGOTE BLUM
Delta Winds ■ 2011
5½ x 5 inches (14 x 12.7 cm)
Mid-range fired stoneware;
cone 6, cobalt slip, stenciled
PHOTOS BY ARTIST

NATASHA DIKAREVA
Memories of Big City ■ 2011
10 x 10 x 9 inches (25.4 x 25.4 x 22.9 cm)
Porcelain, decals; multiple fired,
cone 04-5, underglazes, glazes
PHOTO BY ARTIST

RICHARD BLAKE SHAW
Red House of Cards with Teddy's Poem ■ 2009
18 x 9 x 7 inches (45.7 x 22.9 x 17.8 cm)
Glazed porcelain with overglaze decals

INGRID ANN MURPHY
Lovematch.com ■ 2011
14 x 8 x 4 inches (35.6 x 20.3 x 10.2 cm)
Slip-cast earthenware; glaze cone 4,
gold luster, cone 015, enamel transfer
PHOTO BY ARTIST

IANNA FRISBY
Children Live What They Learn ■ 2004
8 x 90 inches (20.3 x 228.6 cm)
Earthenware, decals; slip cast,
hand painted, silk-screened

GARRY JOHN BISH
Vessels: Right-Angled World ■ 2008

Tallest: 6 ⅝ inches (16.8 cm)
Wheel-thrown ceramic stoneware, enamel
decal; reduction fired, silk-screened
PHOTO BY IAN HILL

323

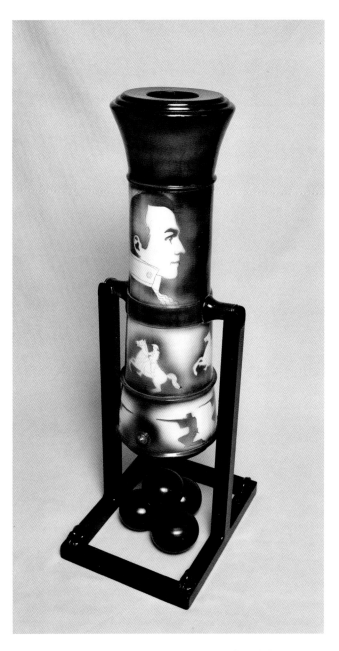

KEITH THOMAS CAMPBELL
From the Canadian Amphora Series: Queenston Cannon ■ 2011
36 x 12 x 15 inches (91.4 x 30.5 x 38.1 cm)
White stoneware, metal frame; multiple fired, cone 08-06,
underglaze, photo stencil, airbrushed, clear glaze, underglaze pencil
PHOTO BY STEVEN NEWMAN

STEVE GARCIA
Smells Like Rain ■ 2009
36 x 20 x 6 inches (91.4 x 50.8 x 15.2 cm)
Multiple-fired slip, four-color decal print
PHOTO BY ARTIST

STEVEN ALLEN
American Pastime ■ 2009
8½ x 15 x 17 inches (21.6 x 38.1 x 43.2 cm)
Porcelain; cone 6, luster, stain,
color screening, underglaze
PHOTO BY ARTIST

SUZANNE SHARPE SIDEBOTTOM
War Ended ■ 2011

3 x 8 x 12 inches (7.6 x 20.3 x 30.5 cm)
Porcelain clay, rubber stamps created from digital images
and photographs; multiple fired, cone 04-5, silver leaf,
underglaze, underglaze pencil, wood-block printed
PHOTO BY ARTIST

327

SHARON ANITA REAY
Oz Bookends: Ozma and *The Patchwork Girl* ■ 2006

Each: 8 x 10 x 8 inches (20.3 x 25.4 x 20.3 cm)
High-fired stoneware, stain; electric fired, cone 06-9,
underglazes, Japanese tissue-paper transfer
PHOTO BY ARTIST

The decal text reads:

> On the
> night before
> *Christmas in July,*
> not a creature was
> stirring; not even
> *"Mama Mouse..."* The
> staff the campers settled
> down for their long
> summer's nap

PAMELA MAE SEGERS
Christmas in July Teapot ■ 2010
10 x 12 x 7½ inches (25.4 x 30.5 x 19.1 cm)
Slab-built earthenware, decal paper; multiple fired, cones
04, 05, and 017, airbrushed underglazes, silk-screened
PHOTO BY BART CASTEEN

329

MARK DANITSCHEK
AMANDA DANITSCHEK
Eucalyptus ■ 2008
7 1/2 x 7 1/2 x 3 inches (19.1 x 19.1 x 7.6 cm)
Slab-built stoneware; electric fired, cone 5, underglaze
monotype print, matboard plate, direct-pressure press
PHOTO BY ARTISTS

THOMAS R. LUCAS
Knot Beaker ■ 2010

6 x 3 x 3 inches (15.2 x 7.6 x 7.6 cm)
Porcelain clay; cone 04-10, photopolymer
with screen-print using wax resist
PHOTO BY ARTIST

GREG JAHN
NANCY HALTER
Hummingbird Taste ■ 2010

5 x 3 x 3 inches (12.7 x 7.6 x 7.6 cm)
Porcelain; high-fire glazes, multiple fired, cones 10 and
017, silk-screened ceramic transfers of original drawings
PHOTO BY ARTISTS

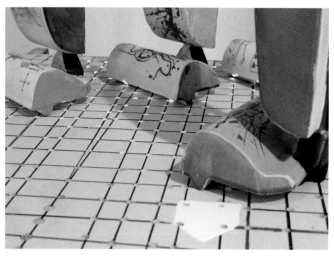

BRETT ALEX THOMAS
Gridsuckers! Featuring the Vacuum-Cleaner Piggy Banks
(Brotherhood of the Traveling Vacuum-Cleaner Salesmen) ■ 2011
60 x 36 x 36 inches (152.4 x 91.4 x 91.4 cm)
Porcelain; multiple fired, cone 6-016, screen-printed
overglaze on glaze, multiple prints, mixed-media assemblage
PHOTOS BY ARTIST

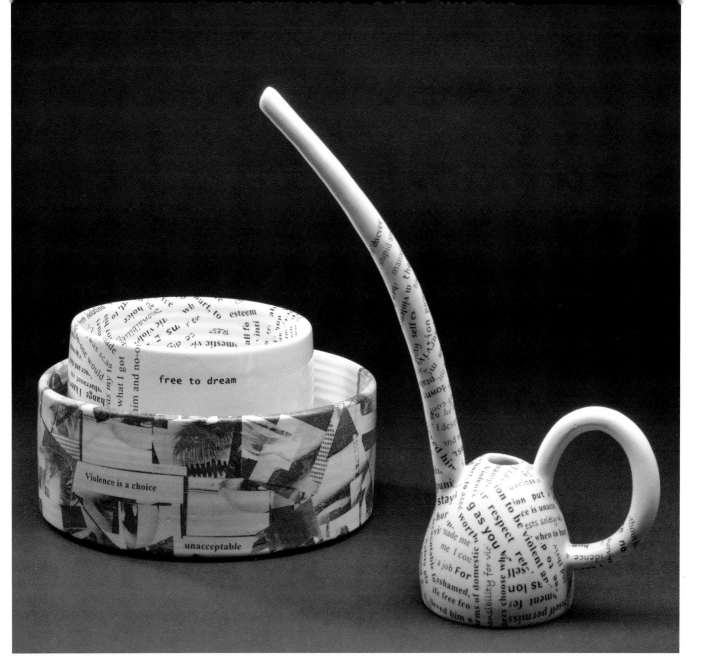

SHIRLEY BATTRICK
Then and Now ■ 2009
14 x 12 x 10 inches (35.6 x 30.5 x 25.4 cm)
Thrown and altered earthenware clay,
artist-made decals; multiple fired, cone 01-07
PHOTO BY DEREK ROSS

REBECCA A. GRANT
Contemplation ■ 2010
15 x 15 inches (38.1 x 38.1 cm)
Earthenware clay, mason stains; oxidation fired,
cone 04, glaze, textured, direct-printed image
PHOTO BY ARTIST

WENDY KERSHAW
Memory Collecting the Flowers Mowed Down by Time ■ 2011
10 9/16 x 11 9/16 inches (26.8 x 29.4 cm)
Porcelain; cones 06 and 6, underglaze, plaster print
PHOTO BY ARTIST

EARLINE M. GREEN
Fulfilling the Dream: Along District Lines
(South Oak Cliff Namesake Panel) ■ 2006
18 x 18 x 4 inches (45.7 x 45.7 x 10.2 cm)
Stoneware clay; bisqued, cone 1, glaze, cone 06,
underglaze, press molds of keepsakes and linoleum cuts
PHOTO BY ARTIST

STEPHANIE OSSER
Pinchus with the Boston Symphony ■ 2011
7 x 13¼ x 8½ inches (17.8 x 33.7 x 21.6 cm)
Porcelain; underglaze, glaze, screened,
carved, oxidation fired, cone 9
PHOTO BY TERESA LATTANZIO

337

THOM O'HEARN
Beer Bottle #3 ■ 2011
11 x 4 x 4 inches (27.9 x 10.2 x 10.2 cm)
Stoneware clay; multiple fired, cone 06-6,
cast object and relief, two-color slip-transfer
print, traced lines, underglaze, glaze
PHOTO BY STEVE MANN

KELLY MCKIBBEN HARRO
Bottle ■ 2011
10 x 5 x 5 inches (25.4 x 12.7 x 12.7 cm)
Earthenware clay, brass; cone 04, screen-printed slips
PHOTO BY ARTIST

KATHERINE M. CHANDLER
Untitled Pattern #5 ■ 2011
12 x 5 x 3 inches (30.5 x 12.7 x 7.6 cm)
Slip-cast porcelain; soda fired, cone 6, glaze,
underglaze, flashing slip, silk-screened, stenciled
PHOTO BY JUDITH EASTBURN

THERESA MARIE SHANKS
Set in Stone ■ 2011
2 x 9¹⁄₂ x 15 inches (5.1 x 24.1 x 38.1 cm)
Stoneware, inlaid local clay on plaster mold; two-mold
process, bisqued, refired, glazed, fired, cone 6
PHOTO BY ARTIST

RAVIT LAZER
Road #443, Human Remains ■ 2010
5 ⁷/₈ x 13 ³/₄ inches (15 x 35 cm)
Stoneware clay, oxides, decals; multiple fired, cone 6-03
PHOTO BY ARTIST

RACHEL LUCIE SMITH
Vase and Dish Set ■ 2008
Vase: 10 x 4 x 9½ inches (25.4 x 10.2 x 24.2 cm)
Dish: 3 x 9 x 2½ inches (7.6 x 22.8 x 6.3 cm)
Stoneware clay, gold luster, open-stock decals;
reduction fired, cone 10, cobalt-oxide monoprint
PHOTO BY LIGHTHOUSE PHOTOGRAPHICS

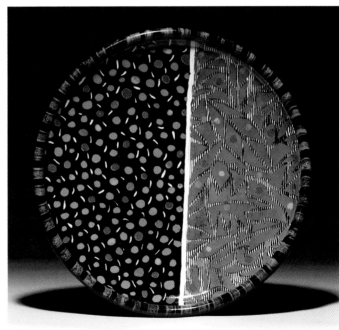

CHARLOTTE STOCKLEY
Untitled Plate ■ 2011

10¼ inches (26 cm) in diameter
Thrown stoneware clay; cone 6,
lithographic print, transparent glaze
PHOTO BY ARTIST

CLAUDIA REESE
Vertical Divide ■ 2011

18 inches (45.7 cm) in diameter
Earthenware; fired twice, cone 04,
slips, stenciled, roller printed, sgraffito
PHOTO BY MATT BICE

ALISON SHANKS
She Just Popped Out ■ 2011
17½ x 16 x 6½ inches (44.5 x 40.6 x 16.5 cm)
Slab-built porcelain, diamante, broom bristles,
stain and acrylic medium; cone 5-6, silk-screened
PHOTO BY ARTIST

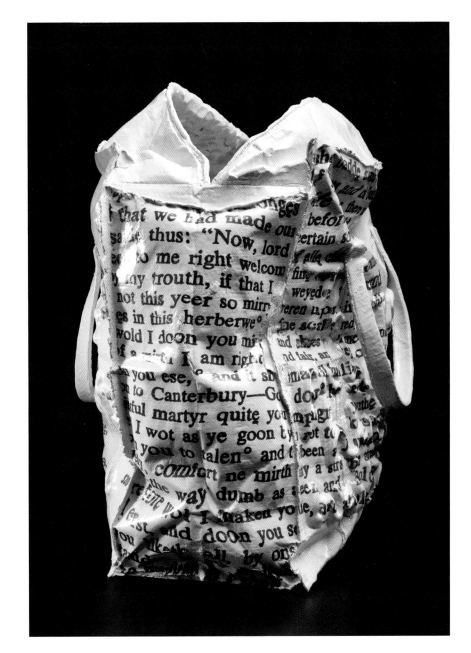

MATTHEW RAW
Moving Stories I ■ 2010
17 x 14 x 12 inches (43.2 x 35.6 x 30.5 cm)
Earthenware clay; black underglaze, multiple
fired, cone 04-01, silk-screened, clear glaze

SUZANNE SHARPE SIDEBOTTOM
Bill Crate ■ 2010
4 x 9 x 12 inches (10.2 x 22.9 x 30.5 cm)
Porcelain clay, black clay; multiple fired, cone
06-5, underglaze, underglaze pencil, stamped
PHOTO BY ARTIST

DALIA LAUČKAITĖ-JAKIMAVIČIENĖ
Tête-à-tête ■ 2009
12¹/₂ x 23³/₁₆ x ⁵/₁₆ inches (31.8 x 58.9 x 0.8 cm)
Manufactured tile, laser-print decals; glaze cone 06,
silk-screened, overglaze colors, lusters, cone 016
PHOTO BY VIDMANTAS ILČIUKAS

347

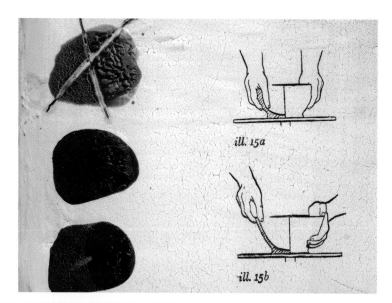

NANCY SELVIN
Notebook Vol. 2 ■ 2009
8 x 13 inches (20.3 x 33 cm)
Terra-cotta paper clay; terra sigillata, underglaze,
screened, mishima, sgrafitto, ceramic pencil, cone 1
PHOTOS BY KIM HARRINGTON

STEVE GARCIA
Hand Signals ■ 2009
15 x 30 x 10 inches (38.1 x 76.2 x 25.4 cm)
Extruded and thrown porcelain, found
objects, laser and on-glaze prints
PHOTO BY ARTIST

RICHARD MILETTE
Teapot with Green and Pink Ground ■ 2001
9 ⁷/₈ x 10 ³/₄ x 6 ³/₄ inches (25.1 x 27.3 x 17.1 cm)
Low-fire white clay, decals, gold luster;
multiple fired, cone 04-016, glazes
PHOTO BY ARTIST

STEVE ROYSTON BROWN
Ripe ■ 2010
5 x 4 x 5 inches (12.7 x 10.2 x 12.7 cm)
Porcelain; fired, underglaze, multi-color
screen-printed, in-mold decoration

ANNA CALLUORI HOLCOMBE
Natura Vita Set ∎ 2009
Each: 11 inches (27.9 cm) in diameter
Commercial porcelain plates, luster,
vintage and laser decals; cone 2, cone 018
PHOTO BY ARTIST

500
prints on clay

AMY JAYNE HUGHES
Nouveau Bleu Platter Series ■ 2011

Each: 13 x 8¹¹/₁₆ x 2 inches (33 x 22.1 x 5.1 cm)
Porcelain paper clay, digitally printed decal, gold luster;
thumb pressed on hump mold, transparent glaze
PHOTO BY ESTER SEGARRA

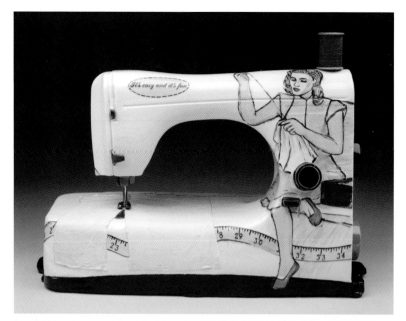

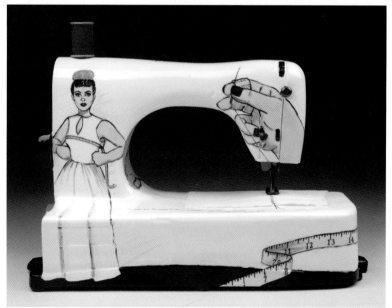

SHALENE VALENZUELA
Sew Very Happy II ■ 2009
12 x 17 x 7 inches (30.5 x 43.2 x 17.8 cm)
Slip-cast ceramic; cone 04, underglaze
illustration, silk-screened print transfer
PHOTOS BY ARTIST

LESLEY BAKER
Vision ■ 2008

9 x 9 x 9 inches (22.9 x 22.9 x 22.9 cm)
Vitreous china, laser and commercial decals,
gold leaf; multiple fired, cone 018-10
PHOTO BY ARTIST

JULIE GUYOT
Untitled Tile ■ 2011
6 x 4 inches (15.2 x 10.2 cm)
Earthenware clay, laser decal; multiple fired,
cone 010-04, underglaze, silk-screened slip transfers
PHOTO BY ARTIST

JESSICA FRANCES SUNSET BROAD
Research ■ 2011
6 x 17 x 10½ inches (15.2 x 43.2 x 26.7 cm)
Porcelain clay, stain; slip cast, cone 6, multiple fired, cone 6-04,
semi-moist underglazes, photolithographic printing
PHOTO BY ARTIST

357

SHARI BRAY
Nefarious ■ 2011
6 x 6 inches (15.2 x 15.2 cm)
Raku clay with porcelain slip surface coat;
bisque fired, cone 04, raku fired in newspaper
reduction, cone 06, underglazes, screen-printed
PHOTO BY KELLY MCCLENDON

MARIA ALEXA COHEN
Nightmare 1 ■ 2010
18 x 11 x 1 inches (45.7 x 27.9 x 2.5 cm)
White stoneware clay; screen-printed underglaze
PHOTO BY ARTIST

359

MEL ROBSON
Veil ■ 2006
3 x 4½ inches (7.6 x 11.4 cm)
Slip-cast porcelain, custom decals
PHOTO BY ARTIST

MOLLIE BOSWORTH
Misty Morning ■ 2010
7 x 5 inches (17.8 x 12.7 cm)
Porcelain, laser-print decal; bisque fired, cone 10,
PHOTO BY ARTIST

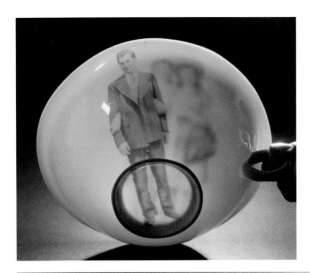

TARA POLANSKY
The Shadow ■ 2008

7 ½ inches (19.1 cm) in diameter
Porcelain, decals; cone 11, glaze
PHOTOS BY JEFF BRUCE

KELLY ANN SCHNORR
Some Day All This Will Be Yours ■ 2010
66 x 48 x 12 inches (167.6 x 121.9 x 30.5 cm)
Earthenware, porcelain, decals, altered
china cabinet; multiple fired, cone 6-018
PHOTOS BY KEVIN FALK

SUN AE KIM
Since Eve Ate Apples, Much Depends on Dinner ■ 2010

Dimensions vary
Bone china, enamel paint; multiple fired,
cones 8, 3, and 011, underglaze, screened transfer
PHOTOS BY ARTIST AND DOMINIC TSCHIDIN

363

MIRIAM RAE-SILVER
Indisposed ■ 2011
9 x 14 inches (22.9 x 35.6 cm)
Earthenware clay; oxidation fired,
underglaze, monotype

DOUGLAS E. GRAY
Scandalous Tweets: Fertile ■ 2011
3 x 10 x 9 inches (7.6 x 25.4 x 22.9 cm)
White stoneware, decals; terra sigillata,
low-fire salt, paper saggar fired
PHOTO BY ARTIST

RIMAS VISGIRDA
TC7 Kecskemet ■ 2010
7 ¾ x 5 ¾ x ¼ inches (19.7 x 14.6 x 0.6 cm)
Glazed Hungarian terra-cotta tile, open-stock decals;
screened image, multiple fired, cone 016, overglazes
PHOTO BY ARTIST

CAMERON PAGE COVERT
Kabuki Edo Fireman ■ 2008
18 x 10 x 4 inches (45.7 x 25.4 x 10.2 cm)
Stoneware clay; low fired, cone 04, multiple fired, laser
transfer, underglaze, ceramic pencil, gloss overglaze
PHOTO BY ARTIST

367

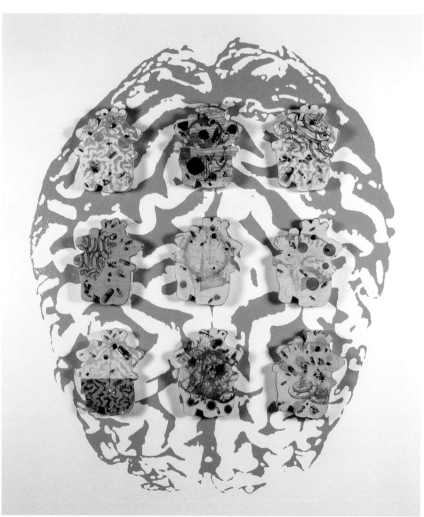

SASHA KOOZEL REIBSTEIN
The Anatomy of Sadness ■ 2010
46 1/2 x 38 inches (118.1 x 96.5 cm)
Stoneware clay, laser-toner decals, vinyl wall decal; multiple
fired, cone 04-6, underglaze, multi-layer screen-print, stenciled
PHOTOS BY JONES VON JONESTEIN

TAL ORA BAR
A Man's Origin Is from Dust ■ 2009
3 ¹¹⁄₁₆ x 18½ inches (9.4 x 47 cm)
Earthenware; underglaze, silk-screened, glaze
PHOTO BY ARTIST

KIK SKAKEL WILLIAMS
Three Small Bowls: Witch,
The Split, and Flying Girl ■ 2011

Dimensions vary
Stoneware clay, decals; multiple fired,
cones 06, 6, and 04, glazed
PHOTO BY ANDREW FLADEBOE

SHARON BARTMANN
Nesting Pitcher/Creamer ■ 2011

5 x 12 x 3½ inches (12.7 x 30.5 x 8.9 cm)
Stoneware clay, original decals; multiple fired,
cones 04, 6, and 04, underglaze, glaze
PHOTO BY PEGGY JO PETERSON

NATASHA DIKAREVA
Searching for Portal ■ 2011
17 x 12 x 17 inches (43.2 x 30.5 x 43.2 cm)
Stoneware, custom-made and commercial decals;
multiple fired, cone 04-5, underglazes, glazes
PHOTO BY ARTIST

AVITAL SHEFFER
Sharkiyah IV ■ 2010
30½ x 21 x 9½ inches (77.5 x 53.3 x 24.1 cm)
Earthenware clay, engobes; glazes,
muliple fired, cone 04, screen-printed
PHOTO BY DAVID YOUNG

500
prints on clay

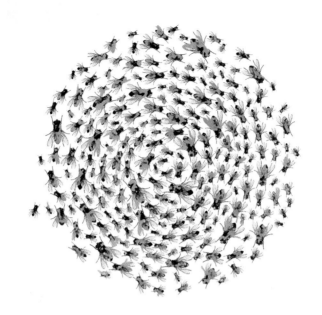

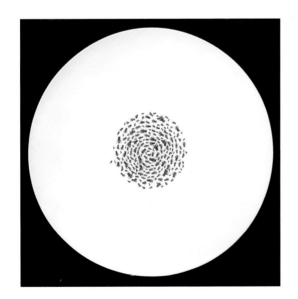

IVAN ALBREHT
Circle ■ 2011

22 inches (55.9 cm) in diameter
Porcelain, ceramic decals; multiple fired, glaze,
cone 1, cone 017, luster, cone 018, digital printing
PHOTOS BY ARTIST

SARA ALLEN
From the Ritual Series: Bow to the House Devil, Street Angel ■ 2011
Frame: 16 x 13 inches (40.6 x 33 cm); base: 36 x 24 inches (91.4 x 61 cm)
Porcelain, oxide washes, photo decal, gold luster, wooden
base; mixed media, multiple fired, cone 017-6, inlaid slip
PHOTO BY ARTIST

STEVE ROYSTON BROWN
Fever Dreams and Earthly Delights ■ 2009
15 x 20 x 32 inches (38.1 x 50.8 x 81.3 cm)
Porcelain; fired, underglaze, multi-color
screen-printed, in-mold decoration

377

BARBARA TIPTON
Built ■ 2009
4 x 3 x 2½ inches (10.2 x 7.6 x 6.4 cm)
Low-fired, sculpture, laser-printed decals;
carved, multiple fired, cone 04
PHOTO BY ARTIST

BETTINA BAUMANN

Heads ■ 2011

Largest: 16$\frac{1}{2}$ x 7$\frac{7}{8}$ x 7 inches (41.9 x 20 x 17.8 cm)
Stoneware clay, decal made by artist; multiple fired, Orton
cones 07, 7, 02, and 16, underglaze, photographed, transferred
PHOTO BY ARTIST

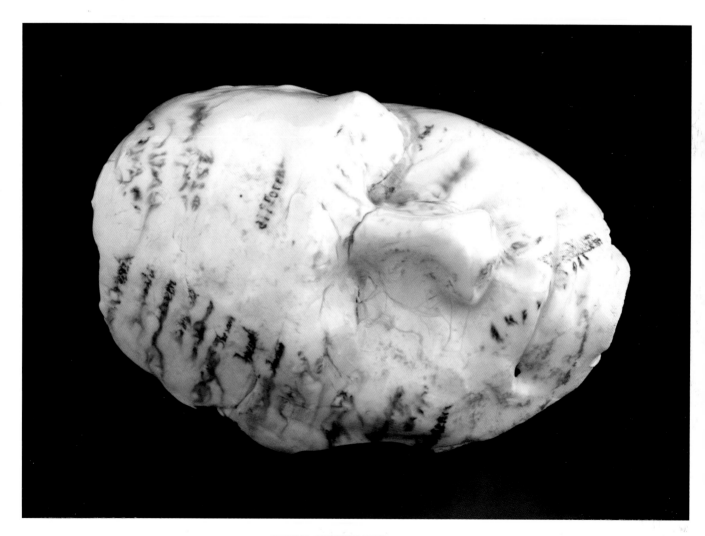

REGINA SCHUHMANN
Repose ■ 2010
6 x 8 x 3 inches (15.2 x 20.3 x 7.6 cm)
Porcelain; cone 10, screen-printed
with underglazes, clear glaze
PHOTO BY GORDON ROSS

MARIA INES VARELA
Reina Vegetal ■ 2010
11¹³/₁₆ x 14⁹/₁₆ inches (30 x 37 cm)
Hand-built stoneware; pigments,
engobes, electric fired, cone 8
PHOTO BY ALEJANDRO GALVEZ

CHARLIE CUMMINGS
Bluehole ■ 2011
15 x 19½ inches (38.1 x 49.5 cm)
Porcelain; four-color separation
silk-screen, ceramic monoprint
PHOTO BY ARTIST

500
prints on clay

KERRY JAMESON
Towers ■ 2007

14 x 12 x 8 inches (35.6 x 30.5 x 20.3 cm)
Clay, found objects, earthenware; multiple
fired, underglaze, glaze, silk-screen on clay
PHOTO BY ARTIST

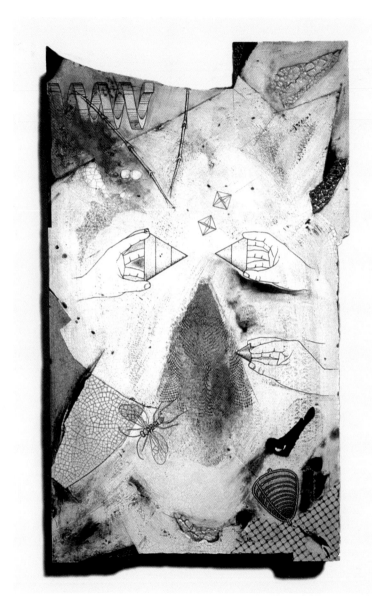

KAREN M. GUNDERMAN
Dexterity (Panel 1) ■ 1998
33 x 20 inches (83.8 x 50.8 cm)
Castable refractory; cone 10 with porcelain
slip, screen-printed stains and underglazes
PHOTO BY ARTIST

500
prints on clay

WENDY KERSHAW
Prepared for Pudding ■ 2011
18 x 6¹³⁄₁₆ inches (45.7 x 17.3 cm)
Porcelain, ceramic decals;
cones 06, 6, and 014, underglaze
PHOTO BY ARTIST

VICKY SHAW
Bowl and Cylinder Composition ■ 2010
2½ x 18 x 4 inches (6.4 x 45.7 x 10.2 cm)
Slip-cast porcelain, red earthenware, black basalt; fired,
cones 5 and 8, press molded, screen-printed underglaze color
PHOTO BY STEVEN ALLEN

MEL ROBSON
Give It Time ■ 2010
Each: 4 x 3 inches (10.2 x 7.6 cm)
Porcelain, stoneware,
custom decals; press molded
PHOTO BY ARTIST

ROSA CORTIELLA
The Collector ■ 2007
58¹⁵/₁₆ x 47¼ x 19¹¹/₁₆ inches (150 x 120 x 50 cm)
Slip-cast white ware, earthenware; electric
fired, 1796˚F (980˚C), silk-screened, glazed
PHOTO BY ELOY ESTEBAN

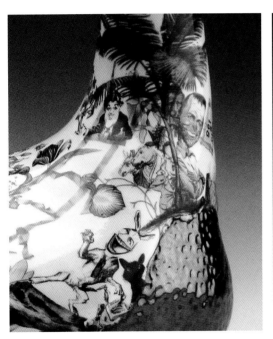

CAROL GENTITHES
The Amazing Goose Chase ■ 2010
16 x 7 x 12 inches (40.6 x 17.8 x 30.5 cm)
Hand-built porcelain, digital images and decals;
multiple fired, cone 2-017, glaze, underglaze
PHOTOS BY ARTIST

389

STEVEN ALLEN
History of War ■ 2008
24 x 18 x 16 inches (61 x 45.7 x 40.6 cm)
Porcelain; cone 6, stain, screening, luster
PHOTO BY ARTIST

STEVE HOWELL
Cutout Platter ■ 1987

26 inches (66 cm) in diameter
Earthenware clay; multiple fired, cone 03-018,
images built up with underglazes in reverse on
plaster then transferred to earthenware slabs
PHOTO BY RANDALL SMITH

391

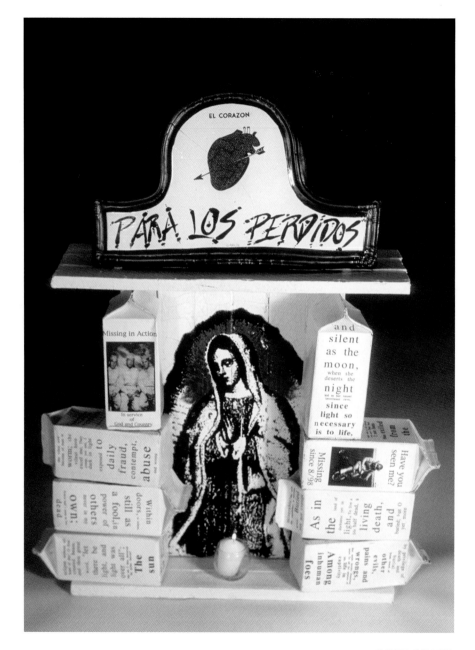

STEVE GARCIA
For the Lost... ■ 2009
33 x 31 x 10 inches (93.8 x 78.7 x 25.4 cm)
Laser-printed images, multiple fired,
cast, hand built, glaze, screen-printed
PHOTO BY ARTIST

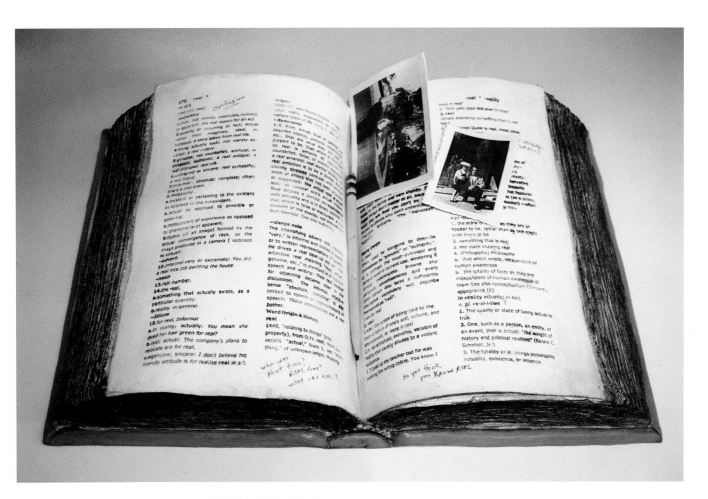

PAULA JEAN MORAN
So You Think You Know Real ■ 2011

7 x 16 x 11 inches (17.8 x 40.6 x 27.9 cm)
Stoneware, porcelain; multiple fired, cone 06-1, underglaze, terra
sigillata, underglaze pencil, Thermofax and photocopy transfer
PHOTO BY ARTIST

RAIN HARRIS
Splice ■ 2009
8 x 21 x 8 inches (20.3 x 53.3 x 20.3 cm)
Slip-cast and altered porcelain, vintage decals,
rhinestones; multiple fired, cone 6-018, glaze
PHOTO BY DOUG WEISSMAN

SANDRA LUEHRSEN
Arizona Valentine ■ 2011
19½ x 19 x 5½ inches (49.5 x 48.3 x 14 cm)
Earthenware clay, artist-designed decals, metallic luster,
nichrome wire; multiple fired, cone 019-03, glazes
PHOTOS BY ARTIST

MARY F. FISCHER
Books Old and New ■ 2011
9 x 8 x 4½ inches (22.9 x 20.3 x 11.4 cm)
Stoneware clay, mason stain; multiple fired,
cone 06-5, copper wash under slip, laser
transfer, etching printed with ceramic ink
PHOTO BY ANSON SEALE

PENNY ERICSON
Toward Milford Sound ■ 2011
8 x 14 x 4 inches (20.3 x 35.6 x 10.2 cm)
Earthenware; fired, cone 02, viscosity print transfer
PHOTO BY ARTIST

DUNCAN AYSCOUGH
Fingerprint on Rounded Pot ■ 2011
5 x 10 inches (12.7 x 25.4 cm)
Wheel-thrown and turned white earthenware clay;
biscuit fired, cone 06, sawdust fired, wax polished
PHOTO BY ARTIST

IAN F. THOMAS
Compensation ■ 2011
18 x 8 x 8 inches (45.7 x 20.3 x 20.3 cm)
Slab-built and molded earthenware, paint,
charcoal; electric fired, cone 02, lacquer transfer
PHOTO BY ARTIST

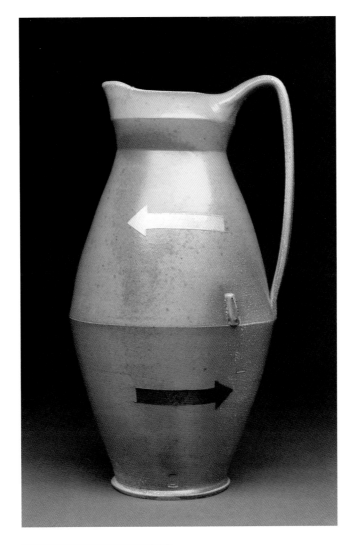

STEPHEN EDGAR HEYWOOD
Pitcher ■ 2008
13 x 8 x 6 inches (33 x 20.3 x 15.2 cm)
Stoneware; soda fired, cone 10, slip stenciled
PHOTO BY ARTIST

BEVERLY CARTER
Tile: Bird Life ■ 2011
7½ x 7½ inches (19.1 x 19.1 cm)
White stoneware; multiple-fired, cone 10 in reduction
and cone 018, screened glazes, ceramic transfers
PHOTO BY CHUCK PAPPAS

Billy looked at the sand-box.
"This is not very funny," he said.
"I will make a new farm.
This farm will have a house.
It will have a barn.
Here are the trees.
Here are the pigs and chickens.
And here are some cows.
Now I have a new farm.
I want Mother to see it."

MARK STEVAN RICHARDSON
Billy's Farm ■ 2005

25 inches (63.5 cm) in diameter
Hand-built earthenware, decals, stains, washes;
underglazes, underglaze pencil, sandblasted
PHOTO BY PAUL MILLER

BEVERLY CARTER
Dunes—Vase ■ 2010
7 x 6 x 2 inches (17.8 x 15.2 x 5.1 cm)
Stoneware; multiple-fired in reduction,
cones 10 and 018, glaze, ceramic transfer
PHOTO BY CHUCK PAPPAS

KEVIN ALLEN TUNSTALL
Fly #2 ■ 2011
7½ x 6 x 3½ inches (19.1 x 15.2 x 8.9 cm)
Wheel-thrown and altered porcelain,
decal; oxidation fired, cone 10
PHOTO BY JERRY ANTHONY

FRIDA MÄLARBORN HOSHINO
Powder Box with Embroidery ■ 2006
2 ³/₄ x 3 ¹⁵/₁₆ inches (7 x 10 cm)
Cast porcelain with cobalt decal
PHOTO BY ANDERS OLOFSSON

The Fibonacci sequence is seen in nature as the arrangement of leaves in a spiral pattern on the stem of plants, in patterns of sunflower seeds, spirals of snail shells, and the number of petals of flowers. The interesting facts are seed heads and the bract patterns of pinecones. The scales of the sunflower is composed of florets which seemingly turn into seeds and spiral also, growing logarithmic, quinangular spirals, moving in patterns of opposite direction, creating this magnificent, unique design.

JUDITH BUSHNELL
THEO BUSHNELL
Fibonacci Platter ■ 2011
14 x 14 inches (35.6 x 35.6 cm)
Hand-built low-fire clay; slip cast, multiple
fired, cone 04-09, laser-printed decals
PHOTO BY ARTISTS

JILL OBERMAN
In Your Absence ◼ 2010
6 x 22 x 2 inches (15.2 x 55.9 x 5.1 cm)
Porcelain clay; graphite drawing transfer
on bisqueware, painted with wax resist,
glazed, reduction fired, cone 9/10
PHOTO BY ARTIST

KERI STRAKA
Catch ◼ 2011
5 x 14 x 6 inches (12.7 x 35.6 x 15.2 cm)
Porcelain clay, gold ring with wire; lithographic
printing, celadon-like glaze, cone 6, oxidation fired
PHOTO BY ARTIST

405

RENA HAMILTON
Oval Serving Dish ■ 2011
3 x 17 x 6 inches (7.6 x 43.2 x 15.2 cm)
Earthenware; oxidation fired, cone 05;
silk-screened underglaze decal, relief slip trailed
PHOTO BY ARTIST

KRISTINA BOGDANOV-ILIC
Join Me for a Ride ■ 2010

Each: 11 inches (27.9 cm) in diameter
Earthenware clay; glazed, cone 04,
underglaze, photolithography transfer
PHOTO BY ARTIST

407

FRIDA MÄLARBORN HOSHINO
Lady with the Lamp ■ 2003
19 ¹¹/₁₆ x 27 ⁹/₁₆ inches (50 x 70 cm)
Ready-made porcelain plates, decals
PHOTO BY ARTIST

MARIA ESTHER BARBIERI
Makiritare Op Art ■ 2007

Dimensions vary
Hand-built stoneware; silk-
screened, underglaze, cone 6
PHOTO BY ANAXIMENES VERA

409

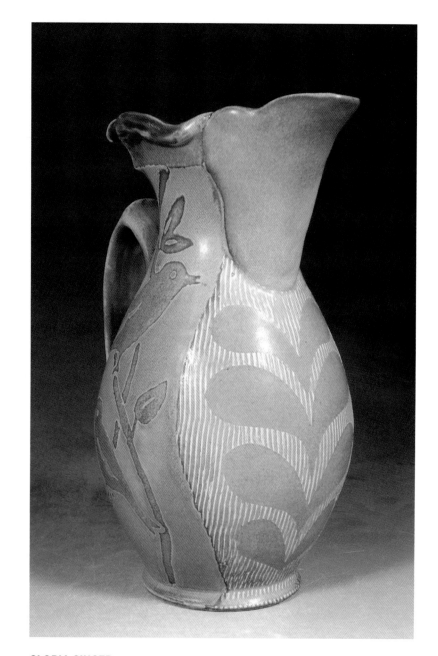

GLORIA SINGER
Pitcher with Birds ■ 2011
10 ½ x 7 x 5 inches (26.7 x 17.8 x 12.7 cm)
Wheel-thrown, altered, and cut white stoneware clay; oxidation
fired, cone 6, porcelain slip using paper stencils, wax resist
PHOTO BY ARTIST

ERIN BETH FURIMSKY
Shift ■ 2009
8 x 11 x 6 inches (20.3 x 27.9 x 15.2 cm)
Hand-built stoneware, decal; Thermofax print screened
with underglaze, mishima, multiple fired, cone 6-04
PHOTOS BY TYLER LOTZ

411

RICHARD MILETTE
Meissen Bottle-Teapot ▪ 2003
14 1/2 x 9 3/16 x 5 1/2 inches (36.8 x 23.3 x 14 cm)
Low-fire white clay, decals, gold luster;
multiple fired, cone 04-016, glazes
PHOTO BY ARTIST

C. NELSON GRICE
Patron Saint of the Spotted Long Neck ■ 2009
24 x 8 x 8 inches (61 x 20.3 x 20.3 cm)
Earthenware; cone 3, underglaze, multilayer
screening, stenciled, relief
PHOTO BY TERRY YARBROUGH

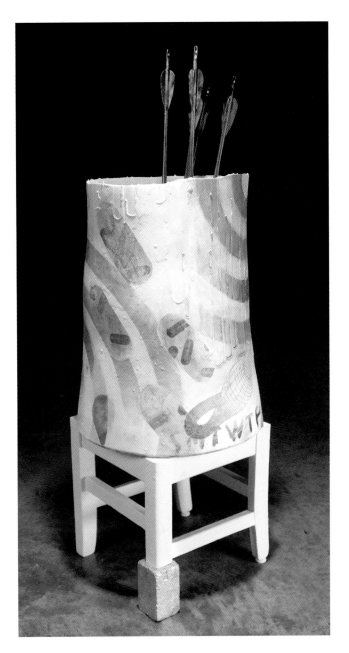

IAN F. THOMAS
The Eagle and the Arrow ■ 2011
40 x 16 x 16 inches (101.6 x 40.6 x 40.6 cm)
Wheel-thrown porcelain, arrows, elementary school chair,
paint, graphite, gilded brick; cone 6, slip, laser transfer
PHOTO BY ARTIST

413

BETH KAMHI
Secret Life of...Words ■ 2008
18 x 4 x 6 inches (45.7 x 10.2 x 15.2 cm)
Hand-formed earthenware clay; embedded text,
multiple fired, post-fire reduction, hand-forged steel
PHOTOS BY ARTIST

DALIA LAUČKAITĖ-JAKIMAVIČIENĖ
Mechanical Things ◼ 2009
Each: 5⁵/₁₆ x 3⁷/₈ x 3 inches (13.5 x 9.8 x 7.6 cm)
Porcelain, decals; glaze, gas fired, cone 11, cone 01,
silk-screened, overglaze colors, lusters, cone 016
PHOTO BY VIDMANTAS ILČIUKAS

contributors

A

Albreht, Ivan Palmetto Bay, Florida 173, 296, 375

Aliberti, Gregory Shaker Heights, Ohio 87

Allen, Melynn Ipswich, Massachusetts 109, 227

Allen, Sara Monterey, Massachusetts 230, 376

Allen, Steven San Francisco, California 326, 390

Altpere-Woodhead, Maiju Canberra, Australian Capital Territory, Australia 117, 267

Amber, Shay Asheville, North Carolina 233

Amikam, Ofra Misgav, Israel 12

Aroh, Beverly Jakub St. Louis, Missouri 285

Aultman, Laura Marie Granite Falls, North Carolina 153

Ayscough, Duncan Carmarthenshire, Wales 398

B

Bacopoulos, Posey New York, New York 63

Bailey, Clayton George Port Costa, California 99

Baker, Lesley Indianapolis, Indiana 74, 105, 133, 155, 255, 355

Banhazl, Terrie Wayland, Massachusetts 49, 103, 278

Baquero, Mariana New Haven, Connecticut 229, 248

Bar, Tal Ora Jerusalem, Israel 369

Barbieri, Maria Esther Naguanagua, Carabobo, Venezuela 161, 205, 409

Barr, Marc J. Murfreesboro, Tennessee 210, 250

Bartel, Tom Athens, Ohio 217

Bartmann, Sharon Ardmore, Pennsylvania 152, 371

Bartolovic, Frederick A. Huntington, West Virginia 15

Battrick, Shirley Mudgeeraba, Queensland, Australia 333

BaumAnn, Bettina Meilen, Switzerland 223, 379

Bayless, Hayne Ivoryton, Connecticut 207, 219

Beyeler, Maggie Mae Santa Fe, New Mexico 288

Bish, Garry John Epson, Victoria, Australia 46, 186, 323

Bishop, Shae Kansas City, Missouri 17, 310

Blackhurst, Chris Rowlett, Texas 258

Blum, Zygote Stockton, California 318

Bogdanov-Ilic, Kristina Delaware, Ohio 78, 407

Bogus, David Scott Laredo, Texas 13, 311

Boldon, Brian Jon Minneapolis, Minnesota 51

Bosworth, Mollie Kuranda, Queensland, Australia 111, 136, 163, 360

Brauhn, Molly I. Clute, Texas 289

Bray, Shari Las Vegas, Nevada 60, 358

Broad, Jessica Frances Sunset Savannah, Georgia 357

Brosnan, Frances Bray, County Wicklow, Ireland 252, 302

Brown, Steve Royston Welwyn, Hertfordshire, England 101, 351, 377

Burnett, Jason Bige Fletcher, North Carolina 42

Bushnell, Judith Seattle, Washington 297, 404

Bushnell, Theo Seattle, Washington 297, 404

C

Calluori Holcombe, Anna Gainesville, Florida 153, 352

Calvert, Aaron Michael Arkadelphia, Arkansas 308

Campbell, Keith Thomas North Bay, Ontario, Canada 325

Carter, Beverly South Dartmouth, Massachusetts 400, 402

Carter, Keith Coral Gables, Florida 171

Chandler, Katherine M. Des Moines, Iowa 339

Chase, Amy Cape Girardeau, Missouri 27, 43, 249

Childs, Dana Powell, Wyoming 269

Cimatti, Antonella Faenza, Italy 59

Clark, Barb Las Vegas, Nevada 257

Cohen, Maria Alexa Voorhees, New Jersey 116, 359

Cohen-Flantz, Tali Ocean Shores, New South Wales, Australia 167

Condon, Judith Nadine Chattanooga, Tennessee 324

Conlon, Matt L. Logan, Utah 19, 142

Cortiella, Rosa Barcelona, Spain 388

Cosentino, Julieta Constanza Buenos Aires, Argentina 279

Covert, Cameron Page Carrollton, Georgia 138, 367

Creech, Nancy San Diego, California 168

Cummings, Charlie Gainesville, Florida 112, 151, 382

D

Danitschek, Amanda San Jose, California 149, 330

Danitschek, Mark San Jose, California 149, 330

Davis, Israel Shawn Grand Rapids, Michigan 93

Debardelaben, Terry Ada Washington, D.C. 104, 192

Debreceni, Robin P. Wenonah, New Jersey 65

del Castillo, Cristina Paso de los Libres, Corriente, Argentina 185

Dezelon, Nicole Marie Pittsburgh, Pennsylvania 300

Dikareva, Natasha San Francisco, California 319, 372

Dowhie, Lenny E. Evansville, Indiana 190

Duvall, Diane C. West Palm Beach, Florida 83

Dye, Carlos Santa Cruz, California 85, 146

500
prints on clay

acknowledgments

To all of the artists who submitted work for consideration and who made my experience as juror so wonderful and so difficult, I extend my sincere appreciation. I reviewed thousands of images, and if a piece didn't make the final cut, that doesn't mean it wasn't strong or appreciated.

A special word of thanks goes to my wife, Jane. Her unconditional support allows me to pursue my artistic adventures. I'm also indebted to my son, Miles, who reminds me every day of what it's like to see the world with fresh eyes.

— **Paul Andrew Wandless**
(Paul's work is featured on this page)

G vs E ■ 2009

about the juror

Paul Andrew Wandless was born in Miami, Florida, in 1967. He holds an MFA from Arizona State University, an MA from Minnesota State University–Mankato, and a BFA from the University of Delaware. He has exhibited his clay work, prints, sculptures, paintings, and drawings since 1995. His pieces are in public and private collections.

A frequent lecturer, Wandless has given more than 60 workshops. He is the author of *Image Transfer on Clay* (Lark Books, 2006) and *Alternative Kilns & Firing Techniques* (Lark Books, 2004), which he co-wrote with James C. Watkins. As an independent curator, he has organized 18 exhibitions. Since 1999, Wandless has taught as a professor at various universities while maintaining his studio work. He has received numerous prizes, including the 2002 Distinguished Young Alumni Award from Minnesota State University–Mankato and the 2007 Outstanding Achievement Award from the National Council on Education for the Ceramic Arts. In 2010, the American Ceramic Society created the video *Fundamentals of Screen-Printing on Clay with Paul Andrew Wandless* featuring his techniques in this area.

Wandless currently serves as Vice President of the Potters Council. He lives in Chicago.

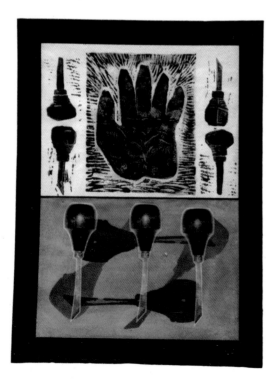

Tools of the Trade #11 ■ 2010

500
prints on clay